Winner of the 2016 National Jewish Book Award in the category of Education and Jewish Identity

Rabbi Mike Uram is the executive director of Hillel at the University of Pennsylvania, one of the top Hillels in the country. He has been recognized by the *Forward* as one of the fifty most influential Jews in America and by Slingshot for leading one of the most innovative and inspiring organizations in North America. He is a frequent speaker on the topics of Jewish innovation and engagement to organizations around the United States.

Dr. Ron Wolfson, Fingerhut Professor of Education at American Jewish University in Los Angeles, is author of *Relational Judaism: Using the Power of Relationships to Transform the Jewish Community*.

Eric Fingerhut is the president and CEO of Hillel International.

Praise for Next Generation Judaism

"Rabbi Mike Uram has emerged as perhaps the single best contemporary Hillel director. While personally modest, he has developed a depth and complexity of understanding of "millennials" that is nothing short of wondrous. His idea of disruptive innovation is but one of many he has successfully employed both at his Hillel and in this book that are truly admirable."

—Michael Steinhardt,
Philanthropist and co-founder of Birthright Israel

"Mike Uram brilliantly studies principles that have informed the Hillel movement in the last generation and applies core principles to the broader communal world. It is done with an effort to recast our community, looking to a future of vitality and meaning."

—Richard M. Joel,
President of Yeshiva University and Former President of Hillel International

"Refreshingly insightful and modest, Rabbi Michael Uram ... experiences at Penn Hillel as well as his vast know ... nal literature, and the American Jewish ... ons in *Next Generation Judaism* for Jewish leac ... : to speak to the current generation of Millennial ... daism into new vessels and explains how existir ... themselves for next generation. This is a uniquely ... ne that practitioners and scholars alike must read!"

—Rabbi David Ellenson,
Director of the Schusterman Center for Israel Studies at Brandeis University and Chancellor Emeritus of Hebrew Union College-Jewish Institute of Religion

"*Next Generation Judaism* is the must-read essential playbook for building a more vibrant, more engaged Jewish future. Mike Uram offers up all of the keys for expansive, dynamic Jewish life--one that will, if we're smart enough to heed his wisdom, absolutely transform our communities and our lives in necessary, needed ways."

—Rabbi Danya Ruttenberg,
author, *Nurture the Wow* and *Surprised by God*

"I was nodding in agreement and internally cheering reading *Next Generation Judaism*. We know Jewish organizations need to change but Mike Uram offers clear, practical and proven guidance on how to actually do it. I want my entire team to read this book."

—Rabbi Angela Warnick Buchdahl,
Senior Rabbi at Central Synaogogue

"Mike Uram has given us a gift: A bird's eye view of how a legacy institution serving the Jewish community can literally re-invent itself from within. I'm all for supporting entrepreneurial efforts to re-energize the Jewish community and engage millennials. But Rabbi Uram reminds us that any Jewish institution is capable of intrapreneurship and he provides a road map for how to get there."

—Rabbi Sid Schwarz,
Senior Fellow, Clal; Author, *Jewish Megatrends: Charting the Course of the American Jewish Future*

"Rabbi Mike Uram has written an important book with major implications for the future of American Jewish life. Mike lovingly challenges the existing models from the perspective that only a truly reflective practitioner can offer. Reporting on the successes that a large Jewish institution had in reinventing itself, Mike offers an inspiring pathway of possibility for all organizational leaders looking to make a substantive change. Mike is a true optimist, and he writes with a vision of a different Jewish community that motivates the reader to apply these lessons far and wide."

—Rabbi Elie Kaunfer, Co-Founder of Hadar

"Uram cogently describes the current Jewish reality, one of broad diversity, multiple identities and communities. He offers not only a sound analysis of where we are at this moment in history, but also an innovative, tested and meaningful pathway (from the college campus) to where we ought to go. The job of Jewish institutions in the 21st century is to support a network of diverse Jewish belief, wisdom, behavior and practice and to celebrate that diversity. A must read for all who lead or aspire to lead Jewish communities."

—Rabbi Steven C. Wernick,
Chief Executive Officer, The United Synagogue of Conservative Judaism

"Mike Uram's forward thinking and expansive take on the work of engagement holds great promise to revolutionize not only Jewish communal life, but also to have a far-reaching impact on government, civil society, and all sectors that inhabit the public square."

—Rabbi Julie Schonfeld,
Executive Vice President, The Rabbinical Assembly

"Rabbi Mike Uram, arguably among the very best Hillel rabbis of our time, offers a compelling and comprehensive new approach to Jewish engagement. Moving from an insightful portrait of the younger generation of American Jews to a conceptually rich yet deeply pragmatic approach, Rabbi Uram graciously challenges inherited wisdom and charts a new path to Jewish Engagement, designed to complement the legacy approach to Jewish Empowerment. The work is provocative, practical, and personal—and needs to be read by anybody concerned about the future of American Jewish life or, for that matter, other ethnic and religious group civilizations in North America."

—Professor Steven M. Cohen,
Research Professor of Jewish Social Policy at HUC-JIR, and
Director of the Berman Jewish Policy Archive @ Stanford University

"In an era marked by uncertainty and opportunity for the Jewish people, in Penn Hillel, Rabbi Mike Uram has created the gold standard for Jewish institutional life. What a gift he has given us by sharing the secrets of his success! This volume is a must read for all those invested in building the Jewish future."

—Rabbi Elliot J. Cosgrove, PhD,
Park Avenue Synagogue

"Our Jewish community is finally recognizing our greatest challenge is also our greatest opportunity - engaging the next generations of young people in reimagining Jewish life, a Jewish life that will become central to their lives. Using his own personal journey and incredible success at the University of Pennsylvania Hillel, Rabbi Mike Uram's *Next Generation Judaism* deeply and thoughtfully examines this challenge/opportunity and is a must-read for today's and tomorrow's leaders."

—Jay Sanderson,
CEO of the LA Federation

Next Generation Judaism

How College Students and Hillel Can Help Reinvent Jewish Organizations

Rabbi Mike Uram

Foreword by Dr. Ron Wolfson

Preface by Eric Fingerhut

For People of All Faiths, All Backgrounds

JEWISH LIGHTS Publishing

Nashville, Tennessee

Next Generation Judaism:
How College Students and Hillel Can Help Reinvent Jewish Organizations
2016 Quality Paperback Edition, First Printing
© 2016 by Mike Uram
Foreword © 2016 by Ron Wolfson
Preface © 2016 by Eric Fingerhut

All rights reserved. No part of this book may be reproduced or transmitted in any form or by any means, electronic or mechanical, including photocopying, recording, or by any information storage and retrieval system, without permission in writing from the publisher.

For information regarding permission to reprint material from this book, please mail or fax your request in writing to Jewish Lights Publishing, Permissions Department, at the address / fax number listed below, or email your request to submissions@turnerpublishing.com.

Library of Congress Cataloging-in-Publication Data
Names: Uram, Mike, 1976– author.
Title: Next generation Judaism : how college students and Hillel can help
  reinvent Jewish organizations / Rabbi Mike Uram ; foreword by Dr. Ron
  Wolfson ; preface by Eric Fingerhut.
Description: Woodstock, VT : Jewish Lights Publishing, [2016] | Includes
  bibliographical references.
Identifiers: LCCN 2016024520 | ISBN 9781580238687 (pbk.) | ISBN 9781580238793 (ebook)
Subjects: LCSH: Jewish college students—United States—Societies,
  etc.—History—21st century. | Jewish college students—United
  States—Religious life. | Jewish college students—United
  States—Identity. | B'nai B'rith Hillel Foundations.
Classification: LCC LB3613.J4 U73 2016 | DDC 378.1/982924—dc23
LC record available at https://lccn.loc.gov/2016024520

10 9 8 7 6 5 4 3 2 1

Manufactured in the United States of America
Cover design: Tim Holtz
Interior design: Thor Goodrich
Cover art: © Jennifer Gottschalk/shutterstock

For People of All Faiths, All Backgrounds
Jewish Lights Publishing
A Division of Turner Publishing
Nashville, Tennessee 37219
Tel: (615) 255-2665   Fax: (615) 255-5801
www.jewishlights.com
www.turnerpublishing.com

Dedicated to my wife, Leora,
and my children Avital, Benjamin, and Jacob
And to my mentor, Jeremy Brochin

Contents

Foreword

Dr. Ron Wolfson

Imagine this scene: You are a professional or lay leader of a Jewish communal organization—a synagogue, a Federation, a JCC, a Hillel, an independent spiritual community, a national support group. You have read the sociological studies that paint a foreboding portrait of American Jews and declining "affiliation." Yet an astonishing 94 percent of respondents in the most recent Pew Research Center study report they are "proud" to be Jewish and 75 percent say they have "a strong sense of belonging to the Jewish people."[1] Like the ever-kvetching people we are, we tend to focus on the negatives: "Why aren't more people joining our wonderful synagogue?" and "How do we get more people to show up at our programs?" and "What do we do about the millennials and their aversion to institutions?" We recognize that "same-old, same-old" twentieth-century models of Jewish engagement are not working as well in this hyperconnected and yet deeply atomized environment of America, but what is the way forward?

Luckily, in the act of opening this book, you have just begun a virtual "coffee date" with Rabbi Mike Uram, the author of this important, challenging, and, above all, optimistic book. Beginning with a clear analysis of the current moment in American Jewish life, garnered from a career filled with many conversations with Jewish leaders, undoubtedly with careful listening to their concerns, Rabbi Uram shares with us all that he has learned about how to invite Jews into a relationship with a Judaism of meaning and purpose, belonging and blessing. As I eagerly turned these pages, I was reminded of a wonderful teaching I once heard from Rabbi David Wolpe when he addressed a group of library patrons: "When I walk through the stacks of the library, I don't see books. I hear the voice of each author saying, 'Open me up and let me teach you what I have learned.'" So grab a cup of coffee and let Rabbi Uram teach you what he has learned: an exciting, game-changing model of Jewish engagement.

If you are like me, as you read this very readable book, you will begin to feel like Rabbi Uram is speaking directly to you. The stories he shares come from real life, not only from the students and staff on campus, but from the many leaders he has met through his consulting and teaching to boards in synagogues, JCCs, Federations, and among his fellow Hillel colleagues.

One of the most important insights in this book of words is that words count. When the target audience is called "unaffiliated," when we label people as "members" or "non-members," even when we talk about "the Jewish community" as if there were only one, when in reality there is a "complexity of communities," this wrong language can lead to wrong strategies. Rabbi Uram offers a more useful terminology: "Empowerment Jews" are those already connected and comfortable in the Jewish space, while "Engagement Jews" are those who could be attracted into a deeper relationship with Judaism, if only those institutions hoping to reach them changed up their approach from "programmatic and transactional" to "relational" (terms I discuss in my book, *Relational Judaism: Using the Power of Relationships to Transform the Jewish Community*).

Revealing the lessons learned from Hillel's outstanding engagement work at the University of Pennsylvania, Rabbi Uram systematically presents a richly detailed strategy for reaching Engagement Jews. Amazingly, he begins by answering the question on nearly every Jewish organization's agenda: how to engage millennial Jews. This chapter alone is worth a year of coffee dates.

The experiences and outstanding results at Penn Hillel are wonderful to hear about, but, rest assured, they are shared in the service of a much larger goal: encouraging mainstream Jewish institutions to adapt the principles of "disruptive innovation" in their own settings. Rabbi Uram convincingly argues for the creation of parallel "operating systems" in an organization, one designed for Empowerment Jews and another—with different branding and strategies—to reach Engagement Jews. He offers useful examples of how this can work in synagogues, Federations, and

JCCs, along with excellent questions for leaders to consider at the conclusion of each chapter.

This brings me to a strong recommendation based on my own experience consulting with leadership groups eager to embrace a relational paradigm: get on the same page ... literally. Read this book together with your fellow board members and your colleagues on staff. Ask yourselves the questions posed by Rabbi Uram and apply the ideas to your own setting. And then, just do it! Teach everyone in your organization how to do peer-to-peer engagement. This will take some courage, some reallocation of time and resources, some risk-taking, and some experimentation. Yet as I have worked with and watched synagogues, JCCs, and Federations embracing relational Judaism, we are already seeing the fruits of transforming the engagement paradigm from programmatic and transactional to relational ... and *Next Generation Judaism* is a superb next step in this important and sacred work of bringing a meaningful Judaism into the lives of our proud-to-be-Jewish Jews.

Thanks for the coffee date, Rabbi Uram. You are a magnificent teacher!

Preface

Eric Fingerhut

One of the central features of American Jewish life is that every element of our Jewish identity is a choice. Whatever we inherited, whatever we learned or experienced in our childhood or university years, we always have the ability to shape and reshape our Jewish lives. Such a choice is a blessing. It means that when we choose to embrace Judaism, to associate ourselves with the Jewish people worldwide and with Jewish institutions, it is a personal commitment, not one forced on us. However we feel about the notion of "commandedness," it is clear that those whose lives are bound up in *mitzvot* do so out of choice and love and see their opportunity to fulfill *mitzvot* as a joy that enhances their lives. This is why the most vibrant strains of Judaism are those that affirm the importance of personal transformation, where Judaism is a gift, not a yoke.

But this freedom to choose is also a challenge to Jewish organizations that have the responsibility of reaching a broad and diverse community of Jews. These organizations—federations, JCCs, Hillels, large synagogues, arts and cultural groups—must build from a base of potential constituents that contains many people who have not yet chosen to affirm their Jewish identities. And many of these organizations are struggling. Why? In short, they can't build community before they build identity. For too long, we have assumed that Jewish identity is ready-made. It's not—and someone has to do that work.

This book by my colleague Rabbi Mike Uram is written to help organizations—and all Jewish leaders and community-builders—reimagine how to engage and build Jewish identity in an age of constant choice.

But this book is not only for Jewish organizational leaders. It's relevant for any leader of a large organization—for-profit, nonprofit, public service—seeking to revise its service model in the face of bracing, disruptive change. The simple truth is that the trend facing Jewish organizations affects every organization—the question is whether we will adapt now, or continue to struggle for another generation or more. If we read this book, and learn from it, we will be in a good position to adapt quickly and not waste the most valuable resource we have—time.

American Jews today choose how many Jewish things they will do and whether they will tie themselves to other Jews. That means that the traditional measure of Jewish involvement—membership in communal organizations—doesn't capture whether Jews are identifying with their Jewishness or whether Jewish organizations are doing the necessary work of engagement. Membership is what happens after Jews are engaged and affirm their identity. Membership is a confirmation of the work that has been done already, not proof that it is being done today.

Consider the case of Hillel, the organization I'm privileged to lead: When I tell people that I am president of Hillel, the most common question I get asked is "So how many people belong to Hillel?" Those who know a little more about us ask "So how many people *go* to Hillel?"

In this book, and through his work, Rabbi Uram has helped to turn those questions around.

The right question is "How many students have been inspired by Hillel to develop or deepen a commitment to Jewish life, learning, and Israel?" Hillel knows that the task of our communal organizations is not to harness a pre-existing Jewish identity but rather to reacquaint young Jews with the blessings of being Jewish each and every day.

For Hillel, the way forward is clear. We must engage young adults where they are and how they are—whether they come from a rigorous Jewish day school background or have no connection to their Jewish heritage. Each student who is engaged by Hillel will learn differently, be inspired in different ways, and be motivated to act by different things. Hillel, like any communal organization, has to offer something to everyone. Not only is Rabbi Uram doing that work, but he is showing us all how to do it as well.

For example, Rabbi Uram's Penn Hillel has divided its potential "customer base" into two distinct groups—Engagement Jews and

Empowerment Jews—and then created two very different organizations, operating under different names, with different strategies, to meet the needs of each group. As described in the pages you are about to read, this approach seems logical, not radical. After all, how different is Penn Hillel's strategy from that of corporations like Gap Inc. that have brands like Banana Republic and Old Navy to reach customers who are seeking different experiences?

Rabbi Uram makes a compelling case that Jewish communal organizations, like for-profit companies, suffer from the organizational challenges diagnosed by business scholar Clay Christensen (and others) under the theory of "disruptive innovation." This theory holds that large, established organizations rarely take the risk of creating a truly disruptive innovation because they are so focused on their current customers who like things the way they are. To translate this to Penn Hillel, Empowerment Jews are already in the building, and they need to be served. Generally speaking, serving them would take all our attention and resources.

How can we do both? How can we engage those who have yet to identify closely with Jewishness while also offering a full-service experience to the already involved?

The answer, for Rabbi Uram—and for hundreds of Rabbi Uram's colleagues serving Hillels around the world—comes from the sages from whom we derive daily inspiration.

When Hillel says it seeks to engage *every* Jewish student in the great saga of the Jewish people, we mean it literally. We know, in the famous words of Rabbi Tarfon, that we will never complete this task, but neither, as the Mishnah instructs, may we desist from it. And we know we can't come close to this goal if we don't innovate and change the way we have been doing things.

No matter whom we currently serve, we must always believe that it is the *next* student we meet who could be the scholar, the rabbi, the artist, or the poet that creates the next chapter in Judaism's love affair with life, learning, and the world.

Hillel the Elder, after whom our organization is named, taught both *al tifrosh min hatzibbur*, "do not separate yourself from the community," and *al tadin et chavercha ad tagi'ah limkomo*, "do not judge your fellow until you have stood in his place." Together, these teachings instruct us to be engaged with our entire community, which includes both those who seek us out and those who need encouragement to identify.

Those who have already chosen their Jewishness and those who have not yet chosen are both indispensable parts of our community's future, and we must be in tune with and serve both. We must not judge those who are not yet involved until we understand their life stories and their reasons for not engaging with Jewish life on campus. Hillel the Elder surely understood that by the time we learn enough about someone else to be able to "stand in her place" we will also know how to connect to them, and will have no interest in judging them.

On behalf of all who are part of the Hillel family, I thank our teacher and our friend Rabbi Mike Uram for producing this important work, and for all he has done to lead our movement. We hope that the Hillel strategies he describes will be useful to many Jewish and non-Jewish organizations seeking to reach those currently unengaged with their organization's mission. We are proud that Penn Hillel, and Hillels everywhere, can serve as a laboratory of innovation for the Jewish community as a whole, and we are committed to continuing to do so in the future.

Introduction

Years ago during a staff meeting at Penn Hillel, we had a conversation in which we tried to define the types of students who didn't feel comfortable in Hillel and how we could engage them in deeper ways. As people began to describe these types of students and the best ways to reach them, I realized something very important: the Hillel staff were actually describing who *they* were in college. This moment taught me an essential lesson about how Jewish nonprofits create strategies—no matter how objective we try to be, our strategies are deeply informed by the personal stories of the various professional and volunteer leaders involved. The methodologies explored in this book are no different. Therefore, I would like to begin by telling you a bit about my personal Jewish story.

Like hundreds of thousands of other Jews, I felt that the organized Jewish world did not meet my needs as I was growing up. I was proud of my Jewish identity but largely disconnected from Jewish organizational life. Aside from my grandparents' German accents and a few Jewish rituals we practiced at home, such as weekly Shabbat dinners (sometimes with matzah ball soup and sometimes with pepperoni pizza), many of my memories of organized Jewish life were negative. Whenever I happened to find myself at religious school or a youth group event, it seemed that the leaders' main focus was on protecting us from or arming us against outside threats like assimilation, anti-Semitism, or bias against Israel. The explicit and implicit message I received was that the essence of Judaism and the Jewish community was to *keep us Jewish* at all costs. We paid very little attention to actually understanding what Judaism was really all about.

In religious school, I learned the basics of what I call "comic book Judaism" and "fortune cookie Judaism." Each Jewish holiday took on a kind of comic book narrative that had a good guy, a bad guy, and a food.

For Passover, it was Moses, Pharaoh, and matzah. For Purim, it was Mordecai, Haman, and hamantaschen. The holidays were about remembering the past but seemed to have little to say about our present or our future. In "fortune cookie Judaism," I learned a handful of aphorisms like "Love your neighbor as yourself" and "To save one life is like saving the entire world." While these inspiring statements are at the very core of Jewish values, the casual way in which I learned them lacked the complexity or nuance necessary to give these sayings a practical application in my adult life.

My experiences with Jewish prayer were even worse. While there was a lot of lofty language about God and spirituality, about sin and repentance, prayer always felt forced, awkward, and stultified to me. As a child, I remember feeling like even the adults were faking it. For the better part of my teenage years and early college experience, I ran from Jewish prayer in any way that I could.

While my family created in me a deep sense of being Jewish, it was not until college that I realized that I lacked the depth of knowledge, skill, and conceptual understanding necessary to make Judaism really come to life. A few remarkable professors and mentors that I met outside the boundaries of a program or Jewish community changed all of that for me. Among others, Professor Pinchas Giller, Rob Goldberg, Rabbi Hyim Shafner, and Rabbi Joe Rosenbloom introduced me to a Judaism that was deep, complex, and challenging. Their Judaism was about more than keeping the Jewish people alive and battling those who threatened our survival. I began to see Judaism in all of its three-dimensional vibrancy. My idea of the Jewish religion was transformed from something that was focused on preserving the past into a living technology I could actually use to live a more full and meaningful life in the present.[1] My conception of Jewish culture grew from lox and bagels to include Jewish literature, music, and art. My understanding of Jewish community evolved from simple ideas about affiliation and "showing up" at programs to understanding that community can be a primary tool for transcending oneself and adding tremendous meaning and value to one's life.

My early feelings of alienation in organized Jewish life may have created a sense of cynicism, but once I was inspired by the substance of Judaism and chose the rabbinate as my profession, these experiences created the basis for my life's work: helping make Judaism more accessible and relevant for all Jews. The fact that I have always felt a bit like a Jewish outsider helps me see my work through a different lens and provides me valuable tools that help me relate to and draw out the stories of countless disaffected Jews.

Many of the ideas, methodologies, and models discussed in the coming pages first emerged from my own narrative but were then supported by the experience of the many Jews who can be described as "post-institutional." They love Judaism. They seek depth and meaning in their lives. But they cannot figure out how to interface with the organized Jewish community.

In addition to my own personal Jewish story, the ideas that form the core of this book were inspired and shaped by the countless relationships, experiences, and intellectual trailblazing of others. In this way, I owe a huge debt of gratitude to the many people who have already contributed so much to help us understand and think about the current reality of the Jewish community as well as those who have pushed us to imagine a different future.

How the Steinhardt JCSC Fellowship Changed Everything

One experience in particular that shaped my thinking about the issues discussed in this book was my year serving as a Steinhardt Jewish Campus Service Corps (JCSC) fellow at Northwestern University. The Steinhardt JCSC Fellowship was a groundbreaking new program started only four years before, with the goal of creating a kind of Jewish peace corps whereby recent graduates who had not been involved in Hillel could spend a year or two working on a college campus to help engage large populations of Jewish students who were not already engaged in Jewish life on campus.[2]

The JCSC Fellowship taught me that Jewish organizations could no longer afford to just serve the people who showed up. The Jewish future depended on going out and meeting people where they were—geographically, culturally, educationally, and religiously.

In the course of my fellowship, I had hundreds of coffee dates with students from so many different Jewish backgrounds. I learned more about the emerging dynamics of American Jewish life from these conversations than I could have from any book or article. JCSC fellows acted almost as anthropological researchers. Each coffee date became a mini–focus group that provided the JCSC fellow with much-needed data about emerging trends among Jewish students in real time and before many in the established Jewish community knew about them.

It was also during that year that I was introduced to the theory of "asset-based community development," one of the central ideas of this book. It happened almost by accident. As part of my orientation to Northwestern, I met with a university administrator who mentioned the work of John L. McKnight and John P. Kretzmann and gave me a copy of their book, *Building Communities from the Inside Out: A Path Toward Finding and Mobilizing a Community's Assets.* In this moment of serendipity, a routine get-to-know-you meeting altered my life and my thinking about how to transform the Jewish community.

Another pivotal moment that year occurred when I was reflecting with my mentor, Rabbi Michael Balinsky, on what I had learned during all of my coffee dates. The main idea I shared that day was that if we really wanted to reach every Jew on campus, we had to do something about Hillel. While the community, the building, and the brand associated with the organization provided a home for many students, it was also a huge barrier and turnoff for many others. I proposed that we start another Jewish organization with a different name that could more easily work with and engage all of those students for whom Hillel just wouldn't work. The proposal never really went anywhere because just a few months later my fellowship ended and I left Chicago for a year in Jerusalem. But the idea stuck with me and would resurface when I started working at Penn Hillel almost a decade later.

When I arrived at the University of Pennsylvania, the Hillel there was already a national leader in developing new models to engage Jewish students who were not already connected to Jewish life on campus. Under the leadership of Jeremy Brochin, director of Penn Hillel; Geoffrey Menkowitz, the first JCSC fellow at Penn Hillel; Rabbi Howard Alpert, executive director of Hillel of Greater Philadelphia; and Michael Steinhardt, visionary philanthropist, Penn Hillel created the first iteration of the Jewish Renaissance Project (JRP), which combined the best methodologies of the JCSC Fellowship with a tactic adopted from Chabad at Penn—hiring students to serve as mini JCSCs to engage their friends. This is what we now call peer-to-peer engagement. In the first few years, JRP was a huge success. Hillel recruited student interns who were linked to populations of Jewish students who were not already engaged by Hillel so that the student interns could bring Jewish life to their friends. As time went on, however, the program atrophied and was eventually disbanded.

During my second year at Penn Hillel, I was asked to re-create the JRP. At first, the goal was simply to replicate the success that had been achieved nearly a decade earlier, but by the second year of the initiative, working now with Penn Hillel's director of engagement, Debbie Yunker Kail, and our new JCSC fellow Matt Susnow, JRP took on a new form inspired by my experience at Northwestern as well as all of the vision and wisdom that Debbie and Matt brought to the table.

In addition to rebuilding JRP as an engagement initiative, we wanted to use JRP as a way of creating a "Jewish start-up," with a separate staff, separate programmatic offerings, and a separate brand. The goal was to run two different operating systems for Jewish life on campus—one in the building, branded as Hillel, and one outside of the building, branded as JRP.

In the years since its reboot, JRP has grown into fourteen different initiatives that now reach over thirteen hundred students each year, in addition to the thousand students reached through the classic Hillel offerings. These two complementary methodologies allow Penn Hillel to reach just over 90 percent of Jewish students on campus each year.

As the success of the JRP spread, some of our thinking and methodology caught the attention of Jewish organizations both local and national. Today the approaches developed at Penn Hillel are active on over 120 different campuses around the country. The Penn Hillel methodology of one organization supporting two different operating systems has won several awards and has become a model for other Jewish organizations that wanted to learn more about it and see how it could be applied to their own work. Since that time, Penn Hillel staff have presented these ideas at conferences, workshops, and retreats for the Wharton School of Business, Hillel International, UJA-Federation of New York, the Philadelphia Federation, the Rabbinical Assembly, the United Synagogue of Conservative Judaism, the Union for Reform Judaism, the Jewish Learning

Venture, and numerous synagogues around the country. After each presentation, both lay and professional leaders often ask for more resources and express a desire for fuller written materials beyond those used in the presentation. This book is intended to fulfill those requests and to share a more fully developed exploration of those ideas so that they can be applied not just to other Hillels but also to synagogues, Federations, Jewish Community Centers (JCCs), and other Jewish organizations that could benefit from a way to engage Jews who are post-institutional in their orientation.

A Note on Terminology and Stories in This Book

Throughout this book, there are certain "dirty" words that I will use as straw men for everything that is wrong with the organized Jewish community. When I use the word "institution," I am trying to conjure the image of an organization that is well established, slow moving, and generally more focused on itself and its own organizational needs than on the needs and interests of its constituents. In these institutions, membership is more important than vibrant Jewish life; program attendance is more important than Jewish experience; past traditions (even if they don't work) override change.

Along with "institution," words like "involved" and "affiliated" will also be used with a negative connotation, not because Jewish involvement or affiliation is a bad thing, but because they become measures of success that assume that the mission of a Jewish organization is to get people to join, show up, or participate, stealing focus from the real work of inspiring Jews to access their tradition in powerful and transformative ways.

In place of Jewish institutions, I will talk about Jewish organizations that are assumed to be faster moving and more mission driven. In place of "involvement" or "affiliation," I will use words like "connected," "reached," or "engaged," which are all intended to connote a set of goals that are measured by the impact they have on individuals and communities rather than how they benefit the institution.

Finally, there are numerous stories that appear throughout this book to help make some of the methodologies come to life. To protect the privacy of the people and organizations described, I have changed their names and locations. In some cases, the only way to keep the story anonymous was to combine different people and situations into one composite story.

Everything Has Changed

I recently found myself sitting in a room full of rabbis at a gathering to help a long-standing Jewish organization reenvision itself. The speaker, Adam Simon, director of Leadership Initiatives for the Charles and Lynn Schusterman Family Foundation, stunned the group with four bold statements. He said:

- There is no longer such a thing as a Jew.
- There is no longer such a thing as the Jewish community.
- There is no longer such a thing as a Jewish institution.
- There is no longer such a thing as a Jewish leader.

Each of these statements was intended to catch our attention and be provocative, but behind the bold pronouncements was something more subtle and more nuanced, something that much of the current sociological and demographic research already tells us. Of course there are still Jews, but the way that identity is constructed today is more fluid than it has been in the past. Of course there is still a Jewish community, but rather than one monolithic community, today the Jewish community is more accurately described as a series of interwoven networks that look and function differently from past communities. Of course there are still Jewish institutions, but increasingly they are struggling to retain the prominence and power they once had as more and more Jews adopt a post-institutional orientation.[3] And of course there are still Jewish leaders, but the model of top-down, frontal leadership has morphed into a model of leadership that is grounded in the power to facilitate and convene.

Despite all of these changes, much of the organized Jewish community is still running on an operating system that assumes that Jewish identity is fixed, that Jewish community is still centralized, that Jewish institutions have the power to decide for individuals, or that Jewish leadership is about leading from out front.[4]

So what should we do when we care about the future of Judaism but things are changing so fast that many of the previous definitions no longer seem to apply? We need help in order to meet these changing dynamics, and we need models that can be applied today to help us get started. That's where this book comes in.

College campuses and Hillels are hotbeds of Jewish innovation. There is a series of conversations and experiments taking place at the best Hillels around the country in partnership with Hillel International that are helping to fuel that innovation and to sketch out what the next generation of Jewish organizations might look like. In the chapters that follow, I will give you an insider's look at what's happening and invite you to join the conversation. The view from campus is a hopeful one, filled with optimism about the Jewish future.

There are a few key assumptions that I want to make explicit from the outset. First, if we cannot find a simple way to talk about the complexity of different types of Jews, it is nearly impossible to meaningfully engage all of those types. Therefore, I want to suggest that it can be helpful to divide the American Jewish community into two major groupings.

The first group has long Jewish resumes and significant levels of motivation to seek out and create Jewish communities and experiences. In Hillel, we call this group Empowerment Jews, because the role of an organization is to empower them to be creators of their own Jewish experiences. We call the second group Engagement Jews. While they may have a very strong sense of Jewish identity, they also tend to have shorter Jewish resumes and to be more averse to Jewish institutions.[5] For these reasons they require a deeper level of personal engagement and more customization from an organization. The vast majority of North American Jews fit into the latter category.[6]

If Jewish organizations want to adapt to meet the needs of Jews given the dynamic and ever-changing nature of Jewish identity in North America, they will need to reinvent the operating system for both Empowerment Jews as well as Engagement Jews.

There is a lot of good news for Empowerment Jews. There are many successful synagogues, Federations, JCCs, camps, day schools, and Hillels that continue to improve in their ability to support and enrich Jewish life for this population. Moreover, we seem to be in the midst of a renaissance that is fueling the creation of myriad new organizations that innovate to improve Jewish life for Empowerment Jews. Organizations like Moishe House (a collection of homes throughout the world that serve as hubs for the young adult Jewish community) and the independent minyan movement are building new platforms to engage Jews in their twenties and thirties.

The bigger challenge is what to do about Engagement Jews who are not getting what they need or want. This population proves to be harder to reach for establishment organizations. There are a few models that are successful at reaching these populations. These include Orthodox outreach groups like Chabad and Aish HaTorah that focus on bringing Jews back to tradition, as well as Jewish start-ups like IKAR in Los Angeles, the Kitchen in San Francisco, and the Kavana Cooperative in Seattle, which are all new models for intentional Jewish communities that have a serious focus on meaningful prayer, social justice, and inclusivity. While these organizations do inspiring work, they are relatively small and don't have enough capacity to meet all the needs of the large number of Engagement Jews. To put it bluntly, this means that a lot of Jews are falling through the cracks.

Engagement differs from outreach in that the goal is not to bring new people in, but to bring Jewish life to people wherever they live, work, and play. It is about bringing Jewish life to people in a way that meets them where they are emotionally, religiously, and culturally.

But this book is about more than just engagement. It's about helping existing organizations that feel frustrated and stuck to find a way, using a different lens, to approach the question of how to engage post-institutional Jews. It's about helping establishment organizations build a bridge between the organization they are now and the organization they want to be in the future.

Why This Book Is Different from Others

In each chapter of this book, we will explore a different methodology that responds to the challenges so many of us in organizational leadership are facing today. We will also explore some cutting-edge ways to help leaders develop the language, the tools, and the motivation to help their organizations adapt and grow.

Rather than trying to report on empirical observations about how to reinvent Jewish organizations, this book will use campus life and Hillel as a case study. Because I am a practitioner, I am able to share an up-close and intimate look at what's working in Hillel and with millennials so that we can explore how those techniques might be applied to adult Jewish organizations. Of course, there are real differences between a college campus and an adult Jewish community. Therefore, using Penn Hillel as an example is not intended to be prescriptive about what other organizations should do, but rather, the work we are doing on campus can serve as a tool of provocation to help organizational leaders think outside the box. In some cases, the models of Jewish engagement that Hillel has developed can be easily applied to Federations, JCCs, and synagogues without much adaptation. In others words, I am hoping that the way Hillel is thinking about its work will inspire other leaders to find their own answers that best fit their particular organization.

I firmly believe that establishment organizations need to engage people outside of Jewish buildings and other institutional spaces. We need to find ways to complement what happens "in the building" by also bringing Jewish life to people without ever expecting them to show up in any particular place. In practical terms, this means that establishment Jewish organizations could ideally run two different operating systems: one for its core constituents who show up and one for all of those Jews who do not. This is a major departure from an organizational mentality that assumes that with the right program or the right incentives, we can transform everyone into the kind of Jew who shows up and wants to be part of the core. Increasingly, the stark reality is that a large number of Jews are post-institutional in their orientation and they are averse to Jewish institutional life.

There is something special about the college student and a college campus. If you spend time on campus with our future leaders, you cannot help but be filled with a sense of optimism. Millennials are smart, talented, and entrepreneurial, and they are reinventing the operating system for Jewish life every day on campuses around the country. Students are not bound by lasting institutional memory or allegiances. In the adult Jewish world, the lines that separate denominations and political and institutional affiliations are more fixed and often impermeable, yet on college campuses, students are able to mix and match in new and creative ways. They are bound only by their own sense of imagination for what the future could look like.

In this way, college campuses and great Hillels serve as the learning lab for Jewish innovation that will shape the Jewish future. Changes that might take a decade to occur in the "real world" can happen in a matter of months at a university. The adult Jewish community can be inspired by and benefit from the vibrancy of what is happening on college campuses today.

A mentor of mine, venture capitalist Marty Lautman, said that innovation requires both incubators that try to develop new models as well as accelerators that can take those ideas and scale them to a larger audience. In this way, college campuses can serve as incubators for ideas that larger, existing organizations can then take and accelerate to help reinvent the organized Jewish community so that it can meet the changing needs of the next generation of Jews.

Finally, this book is a mix of theory and practice that is intended to provoke one essential pivot in the way that Jewish organizations do their work: we need to change the way we do business *right now*, and that change can no longer be incremental. Rae Ringel, a fantastic leadership expert and coach, loves to remind people of the quote "If you always do what you always did, you always get what you always got."[7] The Jewish future requires more than putting Band-Aids on or dressing up current programs, strategies, and organizational structures. It's time to shake it up and be proactive. The Jewish institutional world is already struggling to maintain its position and in some cases even to survive. There are countless outside forces that disrupt the way we are doing business. Let's get ahead of that curve and create our own disruptive innovations.

How to Read This Book

Each of the following chapters is linked to the others. While each chapter can be read on its own, they are intended to be read together and in order, with each one delving into additional perspectives on the central question of this book: how can establishment organizations begin to reinvent themselves so that they are relevant to both their core constituencies and the ever-growing group of Jews who are post-institutional in their orientation?

Chapter 1: Meet the Millennials

This chapter is a concise survey of the current demographic and cultural trends among young Jews, with a special emphasis on millennials—the next generation of Jews, who are entering adulthood right now.

Chapter 2: We Are More Than One Jewish People

When we assume that the Jewish community is monolithic, it leads organizations to think in a "one-size-fits-all" way that impairs their ability to understand and engage different types of Jews. This chapter showcases different tools to help organizations map Jewish identity so that they can develop strategies for engaging different populations.

Chapter 3: Seeding Change from Within: The Theory of Disruptive Innovation

This chapter explores some examples from the business world that explain why it is so hard for establishment organizations to innovate as well as how these challenges can be overcome when organizations seed their own models of disruptive innovation.

Chapter 4: Disruptive Innovation at Penn Hillel

This chapter delves deeply into the way that Penn Hillel, through the creation of the Jewish Renaissance Project, managed to double the number of Jews engaged in Jewish life on campus. By tracing the development of JRP and its methodologies, this chapter will offer a model for change that can be applied to other Jewish organizations.

Chapter 5: Moving from Clubs to Networks: New Ways of Understanding Community

While Jewish organizations often use the word "community," what does it really mean? This chapter explores the power and peril of community as it relates to helping Jewish organizations grow in their ability to reach large and diverse types of Jewish populations.

Chapter 6: Building an Impact Organization

The best way to "keep the lights on" is not to focus on keeping the light on; it is to make a huge difference in the lives of the people you're trying to serve. This chapter explores a series of tools that can help organizations refocus their priorities and measure success in a way that focuses less on building institutions and more on building meaningful Jewish life.

Chapter 7: An Educational Philosophy for Impact Organizations

Building on the ideas in chapter 6 about how to shift the way an organization measures success, this chapter suggests some frameworks for how different educational philosophies can guide organizational leaders in setting priorities and staying focused on their core mission.

Chapter 8: Asset-Based Community Development Theory

This chapter explores how an inner-city community development theory can change the way we think about the challenges facing our community. Rather than focusing on what is wrong, a strategic approach to building on what's right can help us create faster and more responsive Jewish organizations that are much better at reaching Jews on the fringe.

Chapter 9: Peer-to-Peer Engagement

This chapter shows how to take all the theory and really make it work in your organization. Peer-to-peer engagement is the fuel that makes Penn Hillel's JRP model run. Through the art of community organizing and the coffee date, peer-to-peer engagement has the capacity to help resource-strapped organizations dramatically expand the number and diversity of Jews they engage.

1

Meet the Millennials

> Years ago, a Hillel director got into an discussion with one of his
> largest donors. The donor said, "Your fundraising materials only
> talk about the good news on campus, but what about the anti-
> Semitism, the assimilation, the intermarriage, and the anti-Israel
> sentiment on campus? All you have to do is read the Jewish news
> or take a look at one of the annual reports from most Jewish
> organizations to know that we're literally fighting for the survival
> of the Jewish people. And all you can talk about are the outstand-
> ing number of students reached by Shabbat programming, Jew-
> ish learning, and Israel activities. It makes it sound like you're
> out of touch with what's really happening on campus. More than
> that, it's a silly way to raise money. You know as well as I do,
> Jews always love a good crisis." The Hillel director responded, "I
> understand your concerns, but I am actually on campus working
> with the next generation of Jewish leaders, and if I am honest, I
> don't see the end of the world. There are challenges of course, but
> there is also a lot of positive stuff happening, and I actually do
> feel optimistic about the Jewish future!"

While I am not sure if the story ended with an increase in the donor's
gift, the conversation highlights a dynamic that is still alive and well today.
Hardly a day goes by when there isn't a news story or some demographic
study reinforcing the sense that the Jewish community is in rapid decline.
But when you take a closer look at what's really happening with millennials

in general and college students in particular, something more complex is going on. Certainly it does seem that Jewish institutions face an insecure future, but there are also real reasons for optimism about the future of American Judaism. Before we dig into the different methodologies discussed in the coming chapters, it makes sense to first understand some of the demographic realities of what's happening with Jewish institutions and with the major characteristics that define the millennial generation.

Is the Jewish Community in Permanent Decline?

You don't need to be an expert to know that the number of American Jews who affiliate with synagogues, buy memberships at JCCs, and give money to Federations is on the decline. All you have to do is look around at your local Jewish community to see this happening. There are parts of the country where you can drive through neighborhoods and see multiple large and expansive synagogue buildings, but each one of them has a shrinking membership that struggles to maintain the facility.[1] Even during the High Holy Days, fewer Jews are showing up in these institutional spaces than in the past.[2] It's not just synagogues. JCC and Federation buildings are hurting as well.

This is not just a trend in the Jewish community. Affiliation in general is in decline in America today—one in five Americans has no religious affiliation at all.[3] Increasingly, Americans seem to be uninterested in joining a congregation, paying dues, or applying a denominational label to themselves. This is true for college students as well.

In running Birthright Israel trips, Hillels have to interview every applicant and ask a series of questions about their Jewish backgrounds. It is astonishing to see how many of the students, when asked about which denomination they are a part of, respond by saying that while they were raised Reform or Conservative, today they consider themselves "just Jewish."[4] The impact of this trend away from affiliation is just going to expand exponentially as the younger generations move into adulthood. Among Americans under the age of thirty, the number of religiously affiliated young adults has shrunk to 30 percent, the lowest percentage ever reported in a Pew study.[5] Does that mean that people are rejecting religion and becoming more secular, or is something else happening?

There is another telling statistic to consider. Most unaffiliated Americans and 94 percent of American Jews report having positive associations with religion, and most describe themselves as religious, spiritual, or both, even though they don't choose to affiliate.[6] This tells me that the problem isn't religion; it's religious institutions. And this is the key to understanding the positive and optimistic future for American Judaism. We may not be seeing a decline in the Jewish community; we may just be seeing a decline in the institutions that we sometimes equate with the Jewish community. But these are two different things.

Part of what I want to challenge in this book is the assumption that survival of Jewish institutions in their current form is essential. The current structure of religious institutions for American Jews and Christians is a relatively recent development. The current community models for synagogues, Federations, and JCCs are a direct product of the times in which they emerged. The millions of Jews who immigrated to North America in the late nineteenth and early twentieth centuries were culturally and religiously distinct from their American neighbors. They needed safe zones where they could embrace and enact the cultural and religious characteristics that made them different from other Americans. The nineteenth-century Russian poet Yehudah Leib Gordon captured this social dynamic when he wrote that a Jew should be "a man on the streets and a Jew at home."[7] At that time, Jewish institutional space was a physical place where Jews could go to be in their element and be with their people.

More than that, Jewish institutional life was about finding ways to protect and insulate Jews from both anti-Semitism and assimilation. So what happens when anti-Semitism is no longer the same kind of threat?[8] Or when the boundaries between the Jew and the non-Jew become more fluid and permeable? Or when American Jews no longer see themselves as recent immigrants (86 percent of American Jews today were born in America),[9] but as authentic Americans who feel ownership over both American and Jewish culture, even when the two don't align? While no one may have the answer to these questions, it's a safe assumption that trying to fold children and grandchildren back into the mind-set of previous generations is not a recipe for a bright Jewish future. Students, at least at universities with large Jewish populations, don't seem to even understand the desire of previous generations to seek out Jewish-only spaces. Judaism is seen as cool and deep, and students feel that it's easy to integrate all the different parts of their identity in an age that values multiculturalism. For this and other reasons, trying to replicate the Judaism of the parents or grandparents for the next generation is not a good strategy.[10]

Finally, it's important to mention that what's happening to Jewish institutions is part of a larger trend that is affecting all institutions in American life. Following World War II, there was a tremendous boom of community institutions of all kinds, including civic clubs, religious organizations, and political associations. This, combined with the mass move toward suburban living, led to bigger and more centralized synagogues and churches throughout American cities. For the Jewish community, this growth was also fueled by the large number of Eastern European Jews who immigrated to America between 1881 and 1921. They tended to be more communal than religious, and they found these large Jewish communal organizations to be a happy home.[11] It was important for these immigrants to prove to their new neighbors that they were just like them, while maintaining a palatably distinctive Jewish flavor.[12]

But just as Jewish community organizations and civic organizations expanded simultaneously in America, a parallel process is happening now as these types of organizations shrink. Participation in organizations and mass movements is on the decline in many arenas. You can see this transformation in particularly acute ways when you look at the number of Americans attending club meetings during the course of a year. In the mid-1970s, Americans attended about twelve meetings per year, but by 1999, that number was down 58 percent, to just five meetings per year. During that same period, the number of people who went to even one meeting per year dropped from 64 to 38 percent.[13] We see this dynamic play out on campus in all sorts of ways. The following is a particularly poignant example:

> During one of the recent Gaza wars, Penn Hillel reached out to students who were not already engaged in campus Jewish life to help them process what they were reading about Israel in the general media and in their Facebook feeds. We were surprised to find out that almost all of them were strongly supportive of

Israel's right to defend itself. More than that, the students had a very negative response when they learned about an upcoming march to support Palestine. But we were even more surprised to see their reaction to our invitation to join the pro-Israel rally that would also be happening at the same time. They did not, under any circumstance, want to be part of that rally. They said things like "My relationship with Israel is a personal thing, just like my relationship with Judaism," "I support Israel, but I don't think of it like a football game where I need to go to some pep rally," and "While I support Israel, I am not one of those super pro-Israel types—they intimidate me."

This story isn't just about Israel. It depicts the changing way that college students relate to showing up to a large group meeting or event. Their politics are more personal. It's about their beliefs and feelings and not necessarily about showing up to an event or a club meeting.

Establishment Organizations Are Stuck

While so much has changed in the ways that Americans relate to organizations, many Jewish communal institutions still function with the same operating systems they used successfully in the 1950s and 1960s. Many of our organizations still have a strong focus on membership, building formal boundaries between insiders and outsiders, and favoring a top-down leadership model that keeps power in the hands of a few. Meanwhile, according to a Pew Research study, Americans "overwhelmingly think that religious organizations are too concerned with money and power, too focused on rules and too involved in politics."[14] More than that, we live in a world where technology has radically democratized our society. Millennials often feel that they don't need formal leaders, experts, and institutions to get what they want in the way people have in the past.[15] Of course, we still need leaders and experts, but their role in the ecosystem of our lives has changed.

In my experience of working with long-standing Jewish organizations, especially ones that are still doing well by the old measures, there is a real denial of how quickly and how dramatically things are changing. After all, if you are a leader in a synagogue, Federation, JCC, or Hillel that is still thriving, some of these problems are masked by the fact that people still show up, pay for memberships, and donate to umbrella charities. And while it is still true that 31 percent of Jews affiliate with a synagogue,[16] the fact that they affiliate doesn't tell the whole story. It assumes success because they are involved but often doesn't take into account that they are involved only because they have to be—because their children need a preschool, a Hebrew school, or a bar or bat mitzvah ceremony. Affiliation doesn't measure the experience they have while they are members, and it doesn't take into account the fact that many of these Jews carry their feelings of distrust and alienation about the Jewish community with them even while they are connected to organized Jewish life.

What's Happening with Millennials

Millennials are the generation of Americans who reached adulthood around the year 2000. While the exact definitions are somewhat flexible, the earliest proposed birthdate for millennials is 1976 and the latest is 2004.[17] A good standard definition that Hillel uses to understand millennials is the generation of Americans born after 1980.[18] This means that the youngest millennials are in college now, and the oldest are solidly in adulthood. Generation Z follows. While it is worth mentioning that generation Z is poised to create further changes in how our organizations function, I am going to stay focused on the millennials, because generation Z is still in formation and therefore hard to accurately describe.

Whenever I mention millennials to a group of adults, the energy in the room changes. The millennials get a lot of bad press for being self-centered and entitled (for instance, a recent study found that nearly 40 percent of millennials said that they don't like to eat breakfast cereal because it requires too much cleanup).[19] They also create shock waves of fear for many Jewish leaders who are concerned about whether this generation will eventually choose to become members of Jewish organizations and make donations in the way their parents or grandparents did. While it's true that millennials will challenge the status quo, they also present a great opportunity for the organized Jewish world. But before we can understand the challenges and opportunities millennials present, let's get better acquainted with what makes millennials tick.

Some say that they are the "my way, right away, why pay" generation.[20] Millennials expect unlimited options and a high degree of customization for everything, whether it be their food, their consumer products, or even their religion.[21] They have come of age in a world of high-speed Internet and mobile devices, so they expect that things should move quickly and that information should be instantly available at any time, from any place, at no cost. Many of them have also come of age when the Birthright Israel program was already omnipresent and where Orthodox outreach groups are paying people to study or to take leadership roles in Jewish life. As you can imagine, these factors have a huge impact on how they relate to Jewish organizations.

Generally speaking, millennials feel special. They feel they are unique, that their needs and interests are unique, and they expect the establishment world of business and religion to cater to them. They are sheltered, confident, team-oriented, and focused on achievement.[22] This means that millennials tend to be more optimistic than other generations; they believe that they can change the world easily and often. This, combined with their focus on achievement, can also make millennials seem more conventional than past generations. They think their parents and their parents' music are cool.

In general, millennials are more distrustful of people than previous generations. Only 19 percent of millennials report that people can be trusted, compared to 31 percent of generation X, 37 percent of the silent generation, and 40 percent of baby boomers.[23] This distrust also shows up in the way that millennials relate to large organizations. While they love to work in teams and collaborate in more intimate settings, they are suspicious of anything that requires them to trade their individuality for any kind of large "macro identity." They are not "joiners." You see this in the fact that they tend to be brand agnostic, suspicious, and nonresponsive to traditional ways of advertising.[24] Millennials don't want to be advertised "to"; they want to be advertised "with."[25]

Jewish Millennials

Jewish millennials are no different in their distrust of large Jewish organizations, so while many of them want to connect to their Judaism and have noticeably positive associations with Judaism, they are reticent to show it in formal Jewish spaces.[26] They fear that "exploration will lead to exposure of incompetence" or that they will find they don't fit in with the regular crowd.[27] But their hesitation to participate in institutional expressions of Judaism is motivated by more than a fear of not knowing enough or of not being accepted by the community. They also believe that being Jewish is *who you are* and *how you feel*, but not necessarily *what you do*.[28] Therefore, expressions of Jewish affiliation (like joining a synagogue, giving to a Federation, and in-marrying) that were so important a generation ago are less important for millennials.

Millennials tend to prefer smaller micro-communities to larger macro-communities.[29] This is all part of a larger shift in our society from a "Ford economy" built on uniformity, which allowed companies to sell one product to a large number of people, to a "Starbucks economy," where the best companies sell products that feel perfectly tailored to our particular needs.[30] On college campuses, for example, we can see this trend even in the way that students watch TV. Even into the late 1990s students would often gather together in dorm lounges to watch the most popular shows of the day. Today, while students still tend to watch the same shows, they often watch them alone at whatever time is convenient for them, because they can access the shows on their laptops, tablets, or phones. When it comes to Jewish community or Jewish experiences, they want the same kind of flexibility of access. Millennials want diverse entry points that are based in "small, intimate groups; and [that are filled with] stimulating, challenging, [and] enriching content. Big parties and programs that encourage religious observance" are less attractive, according to a recent study from the Cohen Center for Modern Jewish Studies.[31]

Not only do millennials prefer more intimate forms of Jewish community, they also tend to be turned off by any kind of affiliation or membership because that creates a wall between their Jewish lives and the rest of their lives in a way that doesn't reflect who they are. Millennials see their identity as more fluid than previous generations. For example, rather than being either Jewish or American, millennials see their identity almost as a series of windows on a computer screen that can all be open at the same time or that can be rearranged or closed as desired.[32] This means that they don't want to be forced to choose between being members or non-members or between Jewish spaces and regular spaces. They want to feel that their different identity characteristics can be flexible and integrated with one another.

In addition to these broader identity changes, the whole notion of who's a Jew and who's not is changing. For people who might be concerned with intermarriage, I want to share a startling and important statistic: just over 50 percent of Jewish millennials have one parent who isn't Jewish![33] That's half! That means that in most Jewish settings, you cannot assume that everyone is Jewish, let alone that they have two Jewish parents. It also means that one of the simplest ways to determine if your organization is really reaching Engagement Jews is to look at the percentage of your participants and donors who are either intermarried or have intermarried parents. If that number is nowhere close to 50 percent, it probably means that your organization is failing to reach large numbers of Engagement Jews. It is also important to mention that intermarriage means something different than it did decades ago. According to the 2000–2001 National Jewish Population Survey, only 33 percent of children of intermarried families were raised Jewish.[34] Today, for the first time ever, the majority of children of intermarried families consider themselves Jewish (59 percent).[35] This doesn't mean that intermarriage is no longer a challenge for Jewish continuity, but it does mean that collectively we are finding strategies to adapt to this challenge in a way that helps invite more people to stay connected to Judaism. No matter what our personal feelings are about this issue, the statistics do tell us that there is a huge number of people out there who want to feel connected to Judaism but who are going to have a different understanding of the boundaries of Jewish community and the role that Jewish organizations play in their lives.

The other institution that millennials seem hesitant to join is the institution of marriage. While they still get married, they do it later and later. The average age for American women to marry is twenty-seven and for men is twenty-nine—this is up from twenty-three and twenty-six in 1960.[36] Jews, because they tend to be more urban, more educated, and more secular than other American groups, marry even later.[37] It's not just that marriage is being delayed; the process of arriving at adulthood is taking longer than it did a generation ago. The time period between leaving home and reaching adulthood, which now can last well into someone's thirties, is sometimes referred to as "emerging adulthood"[38] or the "odyssey years."[39] Rather than settling down, starting a family, and buying a home after graduating from high school or college, millennials use their twenties and thirties to explore, to grow, and to find themselves. Because many Jewish communal institutions are still focused on serving Jewish families, there is a gap in organizational support for young Jews from the time they graduate from college to the time when they eventually start having children.[40]

While it may feel overwhelming to consider how quickly our society is changing and how dramatically establishment organizations must adapt, times of disruption are also times of great opportunity. The millennials in particular and young people in general are not a problem we need to solve. They are an opportunity for transformation. The key is to remember that we don't have to fix it *for* them. If we can invite millennials to be part of the conversation in the right way, they can teach us and lead the way in reimagining and re-creating the Jewish organizational world. The rest of this book aims to show you how.

Questions for Further Consideration

In surveying the current trends in Jewish life affected by millennials, many hard questions come up about the future of Jewish organizations. The rest of this book is about exploring these questions in a deeper way and starting to find some answers. Below are a series of questions intended to provoke your thinking and prime you for the chapters that follow.

1. What is your organization's experience with millennials? What, if any, strategies have you used to engage them? Where have you been most successful at engaging millennials?

2. What are some things you like about the millennial generation? What are some things you find puzzling or frustrating? Describe two favorite Jewish millennial friends or organization members—of both the Jewishly-engaged and the not-so-Jewishly-engaged varieties. (Keep them in mind as you read the rest of this book.)

3. Given that millennials are highly focused on "changing the world" and finding Jewish experiences that are smaller, more imitate, and more content rich, how would this affect the future kind of programmatic offerings of your organization?

4. How could the idea that millennials tend to want to be marketed "with" rather than marketed "to" affect the strategies your organization uses for marketing?

5. If your organization relies on committees and meetings as a central tool for empowering volunteer leaders, what alternatives might exist for millennials who tend to be less interested in attending and joining such gatherings? Are there other ways to empower people to be creators of Jewish life that don't involve these kinds of formal structures?

2

We Are More Than One Jewish People

A young Jewish woman named Hannah Cohen came into my office, bawling. She had been trying, for many years, to find a place in the Jewish community where she fit, but no matter what she did or where she went, she felt like she was always out of place. Hannah is of Asian descent. She was adopted by an Orthodox family from Chicago. Even though she was raised in Modern Orthodox settings, almost on a weekly basis someone assumed that she was a non-Jewish visitor rather than a regular community member. Hannah also started to question her Orthodoxy. She found Jewish feminism compelling, and she was looking for egalitarian spaces in which to pray. She told me she didn't feel comfortable in either the Orthodox minyan or the Conservative minyan. The final thing she shared with me was that during her gap year in Israel, she had an awakening about what Zionism meant to her. While she still supported the State of Israel, she was very concerned about the plight of the Palestinians. Her family were huge AIPAC supporters and generally right wing in their views on Israeli politics, but she had just started to get active in J Street. She was terrified that "coming out" to her parents as a progressive Zionist would break their hearts.

While Hannah's story is unique to her, the experience of Jewish people feeling like they don't fit in is not. There are so many Jews today who just feel lost amid the Jewish organizational structure. The Jewish community has many different categories and labels, but most of them fail to accurately describe the complex set of ways in which individuals construct their Jewish identity.

And yet, if you scan the brochures, fundraising materials, and websites of Federations, synagogues, Hillels, and JCCs, you get the impression that there is one homogeneous Jewish community to which everyone belongs. Synagogue boards talk about how to get new members to join "the community" or "the congregation." A Federation until recently used the slogan "One people, one community, one Federation." But what does this mean for someone like Hannah Cohen who doesn't feel like she fits in *any* community, let alone "*the* community"? What does that mean for the 50 percent of millennial Jews who have one Jewish parent and who tend to be turned off when Jewish organizations use the kind of binary language that divides the world between Jews and non-Jews?[1]

> "For three years the schools of Shammai and Hillel disagreed.... Then a voice from heaven said, 'Both these and these are the words of the living God.'"
> —Talmud, *Eruvin* 13b

Judaism today is simply more complicated than the "one community" language connotes. Identity is more fluid,[2] people want more customization, and there is a strong sense that being Jewish is immutable, regardless of whether or not a person affiliates.[3] For organizations that want to reach a more diverse group of Jews, there are at least six dangers that come with "one community" thinking:

1. **It's not true.** There are many different types of Jews, who all relate to the Jewish community and Jewish institutions in different ways.[4]
2. **The wrong language leads to the wrong strategies.** When we speak differently, we think differently, and when we think differently, we act differently.[5] Every time we use stock phrases like "the Jewish community," we make a mistake because we fail to acknowledge the complexity of Jewish communities. That mistake often leads

Jewish organizations to adopt a "one-size-fits-all" approach to trying to reach different types of Jews.

3. **It equates Jewish life with institutional affiliation.** Organizations
   need members, participants, and donors, while individuals need
   Jewish experiences, personal connections, and support for their
   own Jewish lives. Sometimes these needs overlap and individuals can get what they need from Jewish life through institutional
   affiliation, but often they don't. In that case, Jewish organizations
   need to find ways to engage people regardless of whether they
   affiliate or not.

4. **It only values Jewish life that takes place inside Jewish institutional spaces.** "One community" thinking often leads organizations
   to only measure and value Jewish expressions that take place at programs and events sponsored by Jewish organizations. In doing so,
   they can ignore and devalue more informal Jewish experiences that
   take place in private or small, informal settings in people's homes
   or other noninstitutional spaces in the community.

5. **It denies people's feeling of uniqueness.** "One community" language lumps many different types of Jews together in a way that
   can make people feel as though the organized Jewish community
   doesn't recognize the different, special, and personal way that they
   relate to Judaism.[6]

6. **It leads to judgmental categorizing.** "One community" thinking
   often leads to categorizing all Jews by ranking them on simplistic
   and judgmental spectrums like "involved versus uninvolved" or
   "committed versus uncommitted." Not only do these spectrums
   tell you very little about what these Jews need and want, they also
   make the mistake of measuring only whether a person does what
   the rest of "the community" is doing.

So if imagining that there is one Jewish community creates all of these
problems, what is the alternative? Do we abandon Jewish community as a
value and adopt a model that favors individuals instead? No. Community
is an essential part of what it means to be Jewish. The problem is not community in general; it's the outdated way that Jewish organizations sometimes understand community.

Jewish organizations can overcome some of the challenges mentioned above if we can develop a new vocabulary for how we think about multiple Jewish communities rather than one single community. This implies that rather than trying to engage all Jews with broad assumptions about how everyone is the same, we focus on a more micro level to learn how different types of Jews relate to Judaism and how those different groups relate to one another. If we can begin to describe and understand the different types

> "It is written, 'All the people saw the voices'—not 'the voice' but the 'voices.' Rabbi Yohanan said: [God's] voice split into seventy different voices, one for each of the seventy languages, so that all nations could hear [God] in their own language."
> —*Exodus Rabbah*

of Jews we are trying to reach, we will be more successful in building the types of organizations that can actually reach them.

Peoplehood and Pluralism: Paradoxes and Possibilities

Yehudah Kurtzer

The paradox of Jewish peoplehood—the argument for the national, collective identity of the Jewish people—is that this same terminology is deployed for two contradictory ideas and their correlating political positions. The peoplehood "industry" tends to connect the idea of Jewish collective identity to Jewish national aspirations, and thus in some circles "peoplehood" is merely a code word for loyalty to the politics of Zionism. In contrast, some of the leading twentieth-century thinkers who coined or popularized the language of peoplehood did so to express the opposite idea—namely, that the Jewish people represented a de-territorialized, decentralized collective, loyalty to which defied the hierarchical and coercive politics embodied in most other forms of nationalism.

Predictably then, if also ironically, this notion of collectivity as encompassed in an ambiguous phrase becomes a site of profound and destabilizing conflict for contemporary Jews. These two interpretations have become caricatures of themselves, the peoplehood industry increasingly shrill in its politics of loyalty and excluding from its conception of "the people" those who do not share those politics; and the non-statist peoplehood ideologues increasingly dismissive of the national dimensions that are obviously so central to what it means to belong not just to any collective, but especially this one with this complicated ancient and recent history. Peoplehood, a discourse of group identity, is more of a contest for various exercises in exclusion.

The elegant way to navigate between these poles and to advance a constructive vision for Jewish community without intrinsic boundaries or obvious rules for discourse lies in appreciating that at the core of Jewish peoplehood is Jewish pluralism. I am struck by a simple line in the book of Esther, one of our people's first articulations of what it means to constitute a collective outside of the easier frameworks of boundaries and sovereignty, when the villain Haman describes the Jewish people as "one nation, scattered and dispersed among the people" (Esther 3:8). In Haman's mouth, this is a pernicious if familiar anti-Semitic trope of inescapable Jewish otherness; as hard as the Jews try, they are essentially infiltrators. In our creative imagination, however, it is a perfectly apt description of what we Jews aim to be: one nation, scattered and dispersed, diverse and diffuse.

Jewish peoplehood could be, if we worked at it, a grand experiment in an unprecedented form of collective belonging, in which the boundaries of the collective were shaped neither by the expediencies of modern nationalism in boundaries and loyalty oaths, nor by other exclusionary frameworks of guidelines, redlines, or even bloodlines. Jewish peoplehood, in this open marketplace of voluntary associations and optional belongings, could be expressed as the composite of those who show up to participate, with loyalty to the collective found in the culturally and piously Jewish activities of debate and dialogue in search of meaning. It is not going to be in consensus politics that Jewish community will be found, much less rediscover its sense of collectivity; but it might be in consensus commitment to collectivity itself. If peoplehood is to be an outcome, pluralism is the technology to make it possible.

Two Models That Free Us from "One Community" Thinking

At Hillel, we have developed two models to help our staff and student leaders to move beyond "one community" thinking and better understand the different ways that Jewish identity functions for the populations we are trying to reach. Hillel as a movement has been addressing this issue since the late 1990s. While none of the models are perfect, they have provoked a series of conversations that have helped Hillel reinvent the way we do business and expand not only the breadth of Jews we engage but also the depth of how we engage them.

These two models are not necessarily distinct from each other. They can be used interchangeably, and they can be layered one on top of the other to help us map Jewish identity on multiple levels and then to think deeply about the different ways that people relate to Judaism.

Model #1: Engagement Jews Versus Empowerment Jews

For decades, Hillel was run as a membership organization whose primary focus was serving members who were willing to pay for programs in the Hillel building. This meant that Jewish life was only for those who joined or affiliated, and Jewish life took place only in the Hillel building or some other designated religious space. By implication, all the Jewish students were divided into two groups: "members" and "non-members." Hillel was largely satisfied working with the Jews who were already active in Jewish life. At the risk of stating the obvious, this same model is still in use today for most synagogues, JCCs, and Federations (donor versus non-donor).

In the early 1990s, Hillel shifted its approach and tried to reach the "non-members" too. Rather than viewing campus as a divided world where there were Hillel members and everyone else, Hillel now tried to benefit all Jewish students on campus. Membership was abolished, and Hillel developed a strategy to go beyond serving just the students who came to the building. Richard Joel, the president of Hillel International, called this "engagement." Hillel's mission was now to bring Jewish life to all students in all corners of campus.

Engagement also meant that Hillel had to expand its role on campus beyond being merely the "shul on campus." If Hillel was going to be able to reach Jews all over campus, it had to integrate itself into everything else happening on campus so that it could also contribute to the overall cultural, educational, and religious vibrancy of the university community. Even today, these ideas seem radical, especially if they are applied to the mission and purpose of other Jewish organizations like synagogues, JCCs, and Federations.

As Hillel expanded its mission, it also developed the new language necessary to describe the different populations of Jews on campus. Rather than thinking of the whole Jewish community as one community and rather than simply labeling Jews as "members" or "non-members," Hillel gave positive, nonjudgmental names to these different groups. There were Empowerment Jews, who were already Jewishly active and who just needed to be given the resources and tools to create their own expressions of Jewish life. On the other end of the spectrum, there were Engagement Jews, who were not yet engaged in Jewish life and who needed Hillel to reach out to them in order to provide some entry point to Jewish life.

At Penn Hillel, we used the language of "Engagement" and "Empowerment" but also added depth and nuances to the definitions to minimize the pitfalls associated with binary thinking. We stopped thinking that our mission was to transform Engagement Jews into Empowerment Jews. Rather than seeing Empowerment Jews as more mature or more fully formed in their Judaism and Engagement Jews as in need of some kind of Jewish intervention, we saw them as two broad categories, each with a different set of Jewish stories, a different set of needs and interests. The goal now was Jewish growth in whatever way was most appropriate for every type of Jew. For Hillel to achieve its mission, it had to reach both Engagement Jews and Empowerment Jews simultaneously, a two-pronged approach, meeting them where they were spiritually, educationally, and culturally.

These categories of Empowerment and Engagement Jews can also be helpful for adult Jewish organizations. Rather than simply trying to figure out how to get the "uninvolved" to become "involved," understanding the differences between Empowerment and Engagement Jews can dramatically improve an organization's ability to reach a larger and more diverse group of Jews.

There are a number of important characteristics that tend to highlight some of the differences between Empowerment Jews and Engagement Jews. Empowerment Jews tend to spend a lot of time with other Jews at work, in their neighborhoods, and in their social lives (we call this exhibiting a *high degree* of Jewish association).[7] Engagement Jews, by contrast, tend to spend more time with people from other backgrounds when they are at work, in their neighborhoods, and in their social lives (we call this a *lower degree* of association). Empowerment Jews tend to exhibit a high degree of Jewish activity and self-direction, while Engagement Jews tend to feel deeply Jewish but don't necessarily feel the need to enact that by participating in organized Jewish life. Empowerment Jews have well-developed Jewish resumes with many organizational experiences that include participation or leadership in synagogue, camp, youth group, Hillel, or Federation programming. They have enough Jewish knowledge to feel comfortable in formal Jewish settings. Engagement Jews tend to have much shorter Jewish resumes and often fear that their Jewish knowledge is not deep enough for them to ever feel comfortable or authentic in formal Jewish settings. When Empowerment Jews participate in Jewish organizational life, they want things like social programs, kosher food, religious services, or an outlet for Israel activism. Engagement Jews, by contrast, participate in Jewish organizational life because they need things like a religious school for their children or a rabbi for a life-cycle event.

It's important to remember that these definitions are somewhat elastic. Not all Empowerment Jews are currently connected to Jewish organizational life. There are many Empowerment Jews who have been turned off or are unsatisfied by the existing Jewish community and have subsequently become unengaged with institutional Jewish life. They are still considered Empowerment Jews because of the depth of their past Jewish activity. The same goes for Engagement Jews. There are certainly Engagement Jews who affiliate with a synagogue or get connected to some other Jewish community organization, but because of their Jewish background, they may still feel uncomfortable or out of place in a formal Jewish organizational setting.

Empowerment Jews	Engagement Jews
Work, live, and socialize with a lot of other Jews (higher degree of Jewish association)	Tend to work, live, and socialize with more people from different backgrounds (lower degree of Jewish association)
Participate in formal Jewish activities regularly and exhibit a higher degree of Jewish self-direction	Tend to feel deeply Jewish but don't necessarily feel the need to seek out institutional Jewish experiences
Have well-developed Jewish resumes with many Jewish organizational experiences	Have shorter Jewish resumes with fewer Jewish organizational experiences
Have enough Jewish knowledge to feel comfortable in formal Jewish settings	Fear that they don't have enough Jewish knowledge to feel comfortable and authentic
Connect with organizations because they want specific types of experiences	Connect with organizations because they need a particular service, like a religious school for their children

Characteristic differences between Engagement Jews and Empowerment Jews.

These categories are intended to be simple and useful. The most important lesson they teach is that Jews are different from one another in more ways than their programmatic preferences, hobbies, or personal interests. Their individual Jewish stories have a dramatic impact on how they view Jewish organizations, and those stories can offer us hints about how to best engage them. Again, it's important to remember that these categories are only a starting point for describing different types of Jews; for them to remain meaningful, there has to be flexibility in how they are determined. Not everyone fits neatly into one category. For example, someone who has spent years active in Jewish social justice activities would be considered an Empowerment Jew when it comes to *tzedek* work but might feel like an Engagement Jew when it comes to Jewish prayer. More than that, even within each group there is diversity. Despite the limitations of these categories, this terminology can still help organizations begin the process of thinking in a more nuanced way about the different types of Jews they are trying to reach.

In order to make these categories come to life, I want to share an example of how we have used this thinking at Penn Hillel. Each week, Penn Hillel runs Shabbat services and dinner that reach four hundred to five hundred students. It's incredible. Depending on the week, there are four or five different types of services, ranging from Reform to Orthodox. The Shabbat dinner that follows is a scene (in fact the student leaders are very proud that Shabbat dinner has been featured in the student newspaper as one of the "scene-iest" places on campus on a Friday night).

On the surface, this looks like a huge success. The building is packed, the food is great, and everyone seems to enjoy themselves. The problem is that when you look a little deeper at who's there, it becomes clear that nearly all of the students who come on Friday nights fit the profile of Empowerment Jews. They are products of many years of successful engagement by the major Jewish denominations. Their families are usually highly active in volunteer leadership activities in their home communities. Nearly all of them have been to Jewish summer camp and to Israel at least once. But what about everyone else? Where are the other two thousand Jewish students at Penn? Where are all of the other students who didn't grow up connected to organized Jewish life? In short, where are the Engagement Jews?

To address these concerns, we began to create new spaces and environments for alternative Shabbat dinners. Now, on many Friday nights throughout the year, Hillel continues to host the regular Shabbat dinners, which are still well attended. But, in addition to those dinners, Hillel enlists an army of student engagement interns (an average of 160 students annually) who host Shabbat dinners for their friends. These dinners take place outside of the Hillel building in dorms, fraternity houses, and off-campus apartments. They are small, intimate, and informal. While the dinners at Hillel are run by a professional dining staff, the dinners held outside the building are run by the students who are hosting them. This is the perfect space for an Engagement Jew. They don't have to leave their friends and venture out to some official Jewish space. They can just get together with their friends and "do Jewish" in their own way and on their own terms.

The different needs and behaviors of Engagement Jews and Empowerment Jews play out in similar ways in adult Jewish communities:

> Imagine Rebecca, a young professional in her mid-twenties who moves to a new city. She's an Empowerment Jew, so she ends up moving to the neighborhood where all the other young Jews live. She knows where to live because it's the same place that many of her friends and acquaintances already live. As soon as she moves to town, she's linked in. She reconnects with some friends from a Jewish summer camp. A college friend is involved at the local Moishe House and invites her to a great Shabbat dinner, where she meets some of her first new friends in that city. Within the year, she gets tapped to join a young leadership program sponsored by the Federation.
>
> Now, meet David. He is Jewish but, in his own words, he hasn't really done anything Jewish since he was "bar mitzvahed." Through his friends and social networks, he learns about a great up-and-coming neighborhood where all the hipsters live. That's where he ends up moving. There are many fewer Jewish people, and it is far away from official Jewish spaces like synagogues, the Federation building, or the Moishe House. Once in town, he reconnects with people he knew from college, but none of them are Jewish. David also ends up developing a great social life for himself. He finds a warm and supportive community, but not a Jewish one.

Both Rebecca and David build on their skills and relationships from past experience in order to jump-start their new lives. Even though they are both Jewish, the way they relate is totally different. Rebecca thrives in Jewish spaces and seeks them out. David is proud to be Jewish, but Jewish spaces feel irrelevant and far away from his daily life and his immediate social networks.

Given those differences, how could the same Jewish organization or program meet both of their needs? David and Rebecca are different people, with different Jewish stories, living in vastly different social networks. So it follows that they probably also need different entry points into Jewish life. David and Rebecca need to be able to be part of different Jewish communities, doing different types of things with their respective peers. So while Shabbat dinner might be an amazing starting point for both Rebecca and David, what that Shabbat dinner looks like, who's there, and what type of food they eat will probably be totally different.

Model #2: Multiple Jewish Intelligences

Imagine you're a teacher in a classroom—let's say a high school history teacher. You love the material you're teaching, and the students are bright and inquisitive. You begin to explain all the ups and downs of the French Revolution. You tell it as a story because the history teachers you had as a kid inspired you with their great storytelling. As you come to the end of the lecture, you focus in on the faces of the students, and you can see that only some of the students are really engaged by what you've said. You pause and ask the class what's going on for them. "This is amazing stuff. Why do you not seem to be interested?"

One student says, "I am interested in the subject, but I just got lost with all the names and dates. I really needed to see it to understand it. It would help me if you could write some of the key things on the board." Another student says, "I am interested too, but I can't absorb everything you're saying. I need a chance to talk through some of it before I can really engage. I learn better when I get to talk in addition to listening."

> "The Torah was given to everyone in equal measure, but everyone chooses to receive it according to their wisdom and their capacity to understand."
> —Rabbi Menachem Mendel of Kotzk

As you imagine that classroom scenario, what strikes you about the comments of the students? (Aside from the fact that these are probably the most self-aware high school students in the history of the world.) They are explaining that they all have multiple intelligences and that no matter how good the teacher's lecture is or how interesting the subject is, different people learn differently and require different types of teaching in order to inspire them.[8] Some learn through listening, some through writing, some through seeing, and some through speaking. Most of them don't fit into one box but require a few different approaches for each subject.

Now imagine what this could mean for how we think about the different ways people relate to Judaism. We know that education is more effective when teachers can understand the different learning styles of students rather than simply labeling them as "good" or "bad," "smart" or "not smart." How much more effective could Jewish organizations become if we could move beyond the simple labels we often use like "involved" or "uninvolved," "Reform," "Conservative," or "Orthodox," "affiliated" or "unaffiliated." By better understanding the complex set of ways that people process their Judaism as a religion, a culture, and an ethical system, organizations can enhance their ability to reach a wide variety of Jews. Rather than simply trying to attract new people by offering more of the same kinds of programs and services, leaders can use the theory of multiple Jewish intelligences to help the organization create a more diverse and finely customized set of Jewish opportunities that could be matched to the different ways that people process Judaism.

Four Dichotomies for Understanding Multiple Jewish Intelligences

The model that we use at Penn Hillel for understanding the different kinds of Jewish intelligences is based on four different dichotomies:[9]

Public	versus	Private
Fixed	versus	Improvisational
Particularistic	versus	Universal
Thinking	versus	Feeling

As I begin to describe each of these dichotomies, pause and try to imagine where you or others in your community fall in each of these categories. Just as there are no preferences given for what type of learner you are in the theory of multiple intelligences, here too, this model doesn't prefer one type of Jewish intelligence over the other. The goal is to better understand and articulate what types of Jewish expressions are most meaningful, most accessible, and most natural for you. So it doesn't matter if you're a "public" Jew or a "private" Jew—both are authentic ways of being Jewish.

It is also important to note from the outset that many of us fall somewhere in between the two ends of the spectrum. Knowing that someone is balanced within one of these dichotomies reveals just as much important information about that person as knowing if someone tends toward one end of the spectrum or another. Lastly, my assumption is that as we try to find ourselves in these dichotomies, our feelings may shift. While it is true that most of us relate to being Jewish in many different ways all at once, my goal here is to ask you to dig deep and reflect on how those different parts of you fit together. My supposition is that upon further reflection, we will find that we have a more unrefined, baseline answer that is the primary way we relate to a given question. As we develop as Jews, we then superimpose additional answers and interpretations on top of that original one.

For example, if I was asked if I was a "particularistic" Jew or a "universal" Jew, my first response would be "both." But if I reflected more deeply on my Jewish story and what really motivates me, my answer would change. In reality, my primary understanding of being Jewish is high on the "particularistic" scale. My grandparents were Holocaust survivors, and a concern for Jewish survival is built deeply into my understanding of Judaism. On top of that, I have learned to love many of the universal messages that Judaism has to offer and now find them to be some of the most inspiring aspects of Jewish tradition. So as you go through the series of questions that follow, I also ask that you try to separate your primary impulses about how you relate to Judaism from the many secondary interpretations that you may have picked up along the way. With that introduction in place, let's dig a little deeper into what each of the dichotomies really means.

Dichotomy #1: Public Versus Private

In what types of situations do you find yourself most engaged and turned on to Jewish experience? When you think about Jewish moments when you feel inspired and deeply engaged, are they in large groups, like standing with thousands of other Jews while the shofar is sounded on Rosh Hashanah or enjoying an incredible Israeli band at a Birthright Mega Event? Or are you most engaged and inspired when you are alone or in a small group, hiking in the woods, lighting Shabbat candles, or praying or meditating alone?

The value of Jewish expression taking place in both public and private ways is deeply embedded in our tradition. There is of course the concept of a minyan—a prayer quorum—which asserts that the most holy and important Jewish rituals are ideally performed in a way that is both public and communal. At the same time, there is also a spiritual practice that emerges from Jewish mysticism called *hitbodedut*, which emphasizes how solitude is an essential tool for accessing the Divine.

The difference between someone who is high on the "public" scale versus someone high on the "private" scale is not just about the size of the group of people; it's also about how they process what happens in that group. So, for example, when you reflect deeply on what makes a Jewish experience special, do you find you tend to want to be with larger groups of people who can lift you up and propel you toward a deeper experience, or do large groups get in the way of that? Do you find that your best Jewish experiences require you to be alone or with just a small group of friends or family? If the group is important, you may be high on the "public" scale, but if the space to be with yourself is most important, you may be high on the "private" scale.

You can begin to imagine how this approach might affect and inform how an organization could deploy different strategies to reach people on all parts of the spectrum. The huge annual Federation party will appeal to someone who is high on the "public" scale but really fail to meet the needs of someone who wants more private ways to interact with Jewish life. In order to meet the needs of both types of Jews, an organization will need to develop spaces that allow for and encourage both the mega party and more private expressions of Judaism.

Dichotomy #2: Fixed Versus Improvisational

When you think back to the Jewish moments when you felt most inspired and engaged, were they moments when you performed a set of traditional rituals, or were they moments when you felt like you were part of creating something new? Is part of what you love about the Jewish holidays the fact that we read the same prayers and eat the same foods year in and year out, or does that formal repetition of the ritual feel tedious and prevent you from enjoying the holidays? Think about Passover Seders. What was the most important ingredient for making your seder meaningful? Was it the fact that you were reciting parts of the Haggadah that are ancient and have been recited by past generations? Or was it that you were able to find new ways to personalize the Haggadah each year? As I ask these questions, if you find yourself more attracted to contexts built on formal ritual and repetition, you are probably high on the "fixed" spectrum, but if you find yourself more attracted to constant change and digression from formal ritual, you are probably higher on the "improvisational" spectrum.

Again, this model can easily be applied to an organizational setting. For synagogues interested in creating opportunities for spiritual expression and exploration, encouraging attendance at services may work only for the subset of people who tend to be higher on both the "public" and "fixed" spectrum. For people who are more attracted to "private" and "improvisational" expressions of Judaism, that same synagogue may need to find ways to encourage, support, and track their ability to help people enact their Judaism alone or in small groups. For this group, lighting Shabbat candles and offering their children spontaneous blessings for that week might be a more meaningful expression of Judaism than showing up for a large service. Again, if an organization wants to engage a wider array of Jews, some kind of parallel Jewish opportunity will be necessary.

For synagogues, this could mean that a new strategic plan would include goal setting for increasing both the number of people attending Shabbat services and the number of people who take on a personal spiritual practice at home. For organizations like Federations and JCCs, it will look different. For example, when it comes to leadership development, someone who is high on the "fixed" spectrum might be perfect to tap as a

---

The tension between the "fixed" and the "improvisational" is also deeply rooted in Jewish tradition. In rabbinic tradition, the word *keva* is used to refer to those rituals and Jewish expressions that are "fixed," dispassionate, and externally motivated, while the word *kavanah* is used to describe Jewish expressions that are spontaneous, emotional, and emerge from one's inner self.

new leader for a long-standing annual program. For this person, the idea of being tapped as a leader to help continue an annual tradition could be a meaningful expression of leadership. Those who are high on the "improvisational" scale might feel this same role is a waste of their time and talent. They might be more attracted to taking a leadership role in something that feels new and entrepreneurial. In this way, the model of multiple Jewish intelligences can even help event leadership development become more customized and more attractive to different types of Jews.

Dichotomy #3: Particularistic Versus Universal

Why is being Jewish important to you? Is it because of the effect it has on you and your tribe, or is it the effect that Judaism has on all of humanity? Are the kinds of Jewish issues you tend to focus on more tribal in nature? Is your focus on matters like Jewish survival, anti-Semitism, and Israel advocacy? Or do you tend to be uncomfortable with a focus only on the Jewish people? Are you more engaged in how Jews and Judaism can contribute to larger conversations about practical wisdom, interfaith dialogue, and justice for all? If you are planning to give money to *tzedekah*, is your first impulse a charity that supports only Jews or one with a large social justice agenda?

For many people, the distinction between being "particularistic" and "universal" is a visceral and sometimes painful one. You can see this up close and personally in the way that American Jews debate how we should engage with and support the State of Israel. For Jews who are high on the "particularistic" scale, supporting the Jewish homeland might be paramount. For those who tend to be more "universal," applying Jewish moral values to the plight of Palestinians could be more central. While most times Jews all along this spectrum value both the existence of the Jewish state and Jewish moral values around human suffering, they differ on which value comes first.

Let's go back to the Passover seder. Is the essence of the ritual to help us remember the story of how we went from slavery to freedom (with a strong focus on peoplehood), or is the purpose of the story to remind us that because we were set free, we must strive to free modern-day slaves from today's Pharaohs? In answering these questions, if you lean toward seeing Judaism as a tool primarily for the Jewish people, you may be a high

Both sides of the particularistic versus universal dichotomy are also found in Jewish tradition. On the one hand, there is Isaiah's notion that the Jews are meant to be *or l'goyim*, "a light unto the nations" (Isaiah 49:6). The Jewish people have a universal role to play in how we express Jewish values in a way that improves the entire world. On the other hand, there is the notion expressed in Numbers 23:9 that the Jews are intended to be *am l'vadad yishkon*, "a nation meant to dwell alone." Some have interpreted this verse as a Jewish prayer expressing our desire to be left alone to be Jewish in our own particularistic way without needing to play a special role in the larger world.

on the "particularistic" spectrum. If instead you find yourself drawn to seeing Judaism as something that has a positive impact for all people, you may be high on the "universal" spectrum.

When it comes to applying this dichotomy to organizations, conscious and intentional voices must be given to the many different points on this spectrum on which people can fall. For example, in Hillel, there is a constant debate about why we run Jewish service programs like "alternative break" trips, where students spend a week or two of their vacation time volunteering rather than relaxing or partying. Is the purpose really to help the people in New Orleans or South America or wherever we are going? Or is the real purpose to use community service as an engagement tool to reach new populations of Jews who are already interested in service? Of course the answer is both. Penn Hillel has learned over the years that to make Jewish service really work for people everywhere on this spectrum, it has to build in time to explore this question and find substantive ways to underscore how service can be both "particularistic" and "universal."

For other Jewish organizations, my recommendation would be to develop programmatic offerings that can work for the greatest diversity of Jewish intelligences as possible. Just as a great teacher finds ways to engage learners who are auditory and visual, a Federation could design service opportunities that focus on Jews in need, for people high on the "particularistic" spectrum, as well as service projects that are focused on all people in need, for Jews who are high on the "universal" spectrum. It might mean that synagogue rabbis consciously build into their sermons material that speaks in both a "universal" and a "particularistic" voice. But even more than that, given the complexity and fluidity of Jewish identity and the increasingly complex definition of what makes a Jewish family, organizations can use this dichotomy to help develop a more sensitive and inclusive language for all of the marketing and promotional materials used by the organization. Rather than assuming that all Jews have the same "particularistic" experiences and tendencies, organizational materials can also make sure to include language that expresses more "universal" sentiments.

Dichotomy #4: Thinking Versus Feeling

Are you most engaged and inspired when something Jewish speaks to your head or to your heart? When you look back at the best sermon you've ever heard, did it make you think or make you feel? When you ponder Jewish ideas about God, what motivates your reaction (either belief or disbelief)—do you tend to first focus on ideas about God or the feelings you have about the subject? The same goes for how you process the power and meaning of Jewish peoplehood. When you try to articulate why the concept of "Jewish peoplehood" is important, is your first impulse to use conceptual frameworks or a more visceral set of feelings? If you are finding that your first answer to these kinds of questions starts with your intellect, you are probably high on the "thinking" scale, while if you find that your primary impulse emerges from emotion, you're probably high on the "feeling" scale.

> The thinking versus feeling dichotomy is expressed in Jewish tradition in the different ways we imagine God relating to humanity. For Maimonides, God is intellectualized and becomes the unmoved mover. God has neither love nor anger. God simply is, and the only way to approach God is through the intellect. But according to Abraham Joshua Heschel, Maimonides is overly rational. The God of the Bible is one filled with pathos. God is full of emotion, of love and anger. For Heschel, the best way to approach God is through emotion, experience, and the cultivation of a sense of radical amazement.

Understanding this dichotomy can be helpful for synagogue rabbis and educators who are trying to figure out what kinds of sermons and education experiences work best for the different types of Jews they hope to engage. Ideally, each sermon and class would have material intended to reach people at all different points on this spectrum. For Federations, JCCs, and Hillels, applying this dichotomy might be a useful way to frame board meetings and leadership development programs so that time is given both to helping people feel inspired and connected to the organization and to challenging them to think and learn at each meeting.

Additional Ways to Apply These Models

There are other important ways in which the model of multiple Jewish intelligences can help organizations to be smarter and more effective.

1. **It deepens your mission.** Rather than focusing on affiliation or program participation, the model of multiple Jewish intelligences helps focus your organization on the goal of Jewish growth for all Jews on their own terms. This also helps your organization avoid some of the dynamics that can make it come across to its constituents as judgmental or agenda laden. Jews on both ends of each spectrum are equally valuable, and their particular matrix of Jewish intelligences is equally authentic.

2. **It changes the definition of leadership.** By recognizing that everyone is different, leaders are prevented from falling into the trap of projecting what they like onto others. Rather than assuming that others will like what they like, leaders can apply this model to help set the stage for building an organization that uses relationships to find out more about what people actually want.

3. **It can help map organizational strengths and weaknesses.** By mapping out both the different types of Jews your organization wants to reach and your organization's strengths and weaknesses, this model can help identify new opportunities for growth and transformation.

4. **It helps contextualize organizational politics.** Often when there are different opinions that arise among Jewish leaders in a board meeting or on planning committees, it is chalked up to politics or

Jews being opinionated. Perhaps it is really just people with different types of Jewish intelligences clashing with one another. This model can help leaders realize that such a debate is not a disagreement that needs to be settled, but an opportunity for the organization to grow and to better cater to both types of Jewish intelligence.

Using American Judaism's Complexity to Fuel Innovation

In Jewish law there is a distinction between dealing with a situation that is ideal from the outset (*l'chatchilah*) and dealing with one that is less than ideal (*b'diavad*). While you cannot put milk into a pot of chicken soup, if a little happens to fall in (less than one-sixtieth its volume), you can still eat the soup. In many ways, when it comes to the fact that we are not "one Jewish people," this may be a less than ideal situation (a *b'diavad* case), especially for those of us steeped in the Jewish institutional world. The future of Jewish organizations would be more assured and simple if most Jews fit into one simple box, but that is not our emerging reality. That said, once we accept and embrace the fact that Judaism in America is getting more complex, we can move forward and realize that if we can push our organizations to adapt, this complexity can also fuel countless new opportunities for making Jewish life more vibrant than ever.

That brighter Jewish future will require organizations to develop more than just multiple programmatic options; they will need to use different methodologies that can engage a wide variety of Jewish intelligences in a richer set of Jewish opportunities.

Questions for Further Consideration

1. When you look at who your organization currently reaches and who they could reach, who fits into the Empowerment category, and who fits into the Engagement one?

2. In looking at your organizational mission and your aspirational vision, what kind of time and resources would you ideally want to commit to working with both Engagement and Empowerment Jews?

3. Does your organization currently have different strategies and initiatives for working with these different groups? If so, what are they? If not, why not?

4. Based on descriptions above, how would a strategy for reaching Engagement Jews look different from what you currently do? How would it look the same?

5. When you look at the regulars or leaders in your organization, do you think they represent people who express all different types of Jewish intelligence?

6. If you were to rank your current programmatic offerings and leadership opportunities based on the theory of multiple Jewish intelligences, which types of intelligence do you currently engage successfully, and which ones might require new strategies?

3

Seeding Change from Within

The Theory of Disruptive Innovation

In a Midwestern city, there was a well-established synagogue that was known for being a warm and down-to-earth congregation. Their biggest challenge was location. While the Jewish community kept moving east, their building was located on the western edge of the neighborhood where the Jewish community had settled twenty or thirty years ago. By most measures the congregation was healthy, and many "regulars" who lived nearby were happy to stay involved. But as the years went by, that dynamic changed. The membership was aging, and new families were not replacing the older ones. The building was aging, too, and getting more expensive to maintain each year.

The leadership realized that some kind of change was necessary if there were to be a long-term future for the synagogue. As they discussed potential strategies for change, an opportunity arose. A new plot of land much farther east, right in the center of where the new Jewish community was emerging, was up for sale. If they moved quickly, they would be the first denominational synagogue to open there and would have first crack at all the young families. While the leadership recognized this opportunity, many members of the congregation resisted the idea of moving. They had a space and a community that they loved, that felt familiar, and that met their needs. After many months of tense meetings and debate, the leadership decided to play it safe. Rather than moving to the new neighborhood, they decided to renovate their existing building and launch a new marketing campaign to try to attract new members.

This story doesn't end well. The renovations cost more money than the shrinking congregation had to spend. The updated facility and new marketing campaign didn't attract the new members they wanted. Things got worse and worse until finally the congregation had to move. But by the time they finally made the move east, they had already missed their opportunity—property values in both neighborhoods had changed significantly. They ended up selling the original property for much less than they expected, while having to pay more for the new land than they ever imagined. In addition to the financial pitfalls of this less-than-ideal timing, they had lost the competitive edge that would have come with being the first synagogue in the emerging neighborhood and now needed to compete with other congregations.

What happened here? Why was it so hard for this establishment organization to change, adapt, and innovate? Was it bad leadership? Was it congregational dysfunction? Maybe in part, but it was also something else. This organization was stuck, trapped in a dynamic called the "innovator's dilemma": its mature and healthy practices for sustaining the current situation were so ingrained that it could not pivot in a new direction when change was needed.

While this story provides a dramatic example of an organization that is stuck, there are versions of this happening every day in different Hillels, synagogues, Federations, and JCCs in so many different Jewish communities. High Holy Day services at synagogues all around the country lack the meaning and vibrancy that both congregants and clergy want, and yet change is slow. Federations know that the trend in philanthropy is moving away from giving to umbrella organizations, and yet what would a Federation look like if it were to try to get ahead of that trend?

"Why does the Torah teach that 'Moses *caused* Israel to set out from the Sea of Reeds (Exodus 15:22)'? Moses had to drag them away from Egypt. Why? They didn't want to leave. Even though their current situation was bad, they didn't want to change."

—Adapted from Midrash *Tanhuma*

The world is changing incredibly fast. As we have discussed, the very nature of how Jewish identity is created and how Jews relate to organizations is in flux. If the establishment organizations of the American Jewish community want to remain vital, change will be necessary. But how? How can organizations that were built on one operating system find ways to experiment with new models and then apply and scale the ones that work best?

There is a way to do this, but it requires an honest conversation about the limitations of the current models we have for Jewish organizations as well as some willingness to take new risks. This chapter will focus on the innovator's dilemma and try to better understand why it's so hard for establishment organizations to change and how this dynamic has been overcome in the business world.[1]

Defining the Innovator's Dilemma

Many companies seem to do everything right and yet end up being eclipsed by new companies and new technologies. Why is it so common for great companies that are well managed to grow and succeed to a point that they settle into an establishment position that prevents them from being truly innovative?

A great example of this phenomenon is Kodak. At the height of its power, Kodak employed more than 140,000 people and had a market value of $28 billion.[2] They were considered an unshakable blue-chip stock. Their marketing and branding were so powerful that even today people take photos and call them "Kodak moments," even though they're using a cell phone to snap a digital image. In 1975, Kodak actually developed the technology for the digital camera that eventually destroyed the market for their core business, which relied on film and photo paper. The company just could not adapt nimbly enough to harness the power of this new technology. By 2012, Kodak had filed for bankruptcy, while digital photography continued to thrive. This story about an establishment firm being overturned by a disruptive innovation is just one among many. So what happened here? Why do otherwise well-run companies that specialize in producing high-quality products get overtaken by less-organized start-ups that may initially offer inferior products?

In part, this happens because the core competencies that are required to manage large organizations are fundamentally different from those required to innovate. Large companies need smart, careful, and thoughtful managers. Before taking risks, they engage in thorough research and comprehensive internal processes to bring stakeholders along. They are responsive to the needs and interests of the customers and investors who make up their core markets. In other words, the managers of these solid companies "play the game" the way they are supposed to and follow all of the "best practices" in the field, and yet their companies are overtaken by start-ups armed with more innovative technology.[3] When management "plays the game" the right way and follows all of the "best practices," they are doing more than just building an organizational model that is highly stable and safe; they are also building an organization that can change only in limited and incremental ways.

The same dynamic is found in the Jewish organizational world. The core competencies that are required to run large synagogues, Federations, JCCs, and denominations make it much harder for them to innovate. They do everything right. They run organizations that are efficient, produce quality programmatic offerings, and have highly developed internal processes that rival those of well-run for-profit companies. And yet, they are struggling to adapt to the changing nature of the Jewish community in America.

Sustaining Technologies Versus Disruptive Technologies

Establishment organizations tend to employ "sustaining technologies," while engagement organizations tend toward "disruptive technologies."

Before I define these terms, consider the following example, which illustrates the distinction:

> Both a large, established synagogue and a start-up minyan are looking for new cantors. While the leaders of the synagogue would ideally like to hire someone who could shake things up and enliven their community, they still need a cantor who will perform all the usual tasks beyond leading services, including bar/bat mitzvah tutoring, committee work, and community engagement. They must also adhere to the rules of their denomination for hiring, which limits the pool from which they can interview candidates. In the end, the synagogue must hire someone who can maintain the status quo. The new minyan, however, has a smaller, more uniform constituency. They don't have a previous cantor to whom their members will compare new candidates, and they are not beholden to any denominational institutions, so they can hire anyone they like, regardless of his or her background.

The synagogue from the example above hires an amazing cantor who sustains the congregation, while the start-up hires a musician with a great Jewish background but no formal cantorial training. Her resume alone disrupts what it means to be a cantor. Just because of her different set of life experiences and lack of formal training, she changes how music and prayer work in the minyan. Both organizations may have ended up hiring fantastic cantors, but the role they will each play in their congregation is fundamentally different.

"Services are conducted with dignity and precision. The rendition of the liturgy is smooth. Everything is present: decorum, voice, ceremony. But one thing is missing: *life*."

—Abraham Joshua Heschel

Sustaining technologies are well-designed, high-quality tools that establishment companies develop to maintain their market share and meet the existing needs of their customers.[4] In the Jewish organizational world, this may be analogous to High Holy Day services that are well attended and professionally executed, a new Jewish learning program run by the Federation for leaders who are already active in Jewish life, or a new BBYO community service program rolled out across the country. These programs are successful in terms of the numbers of people who participate and enjoy them. They are not, however, transformative to people's Jewish lives—meaning that while people may enjoy them, these programs do not radically affect the Jewish feelings, behaviors, or knowledge base of their participants. More than that, these programs tend to attract only people who are already participants or consumers of institutional Jewish life (otherwise known as Empowerment Jews).

Disruptive technologies, in contrast, are those that upset the establishment and essentially change everything—they have the power to disrupt the way that people do business or live their lives.[5]

> A great example of a disruptive technology was the advent of the MP3 format—a digital music file. The music industry was drunk on CDs. They were viewed by many in the industry as an almost messianic savior from older, clunky predecessors like the 8-track, the record, and the cassette tape. They were cheap and easy to make and no matter how many were printed, there was always uniform sound quality. The leaders of the music business saw no end in sight for their increasing sales and skyrocketing profits. So in 1998 Seagram bought Polygram (a large manufacturer of CDs) and merged it with Universal, their music division, so they could enjoy an even larger share of these soaring profits. As soon as the acquisition was complete, the executives at Universal invested millions to upgrade their production capability, producing a half-million CDs per day. What the executives didn't know is that while they were upgrading their ability to manufacture CDs, people were beginning to experiment with MP3s—a technology that would ultimately render CDs obsolete. The great and tragic irony of this story is that among the people tinkering with MP3s in those early days was a man named Bennie Glover, who worked at Polygram in the CD manufacturing department. By day he was producing CDs, and by night he was helping to develop the technology that would destroy them.[6]

In Judaism, there are many examples of disruptive innovation as well. There are classical examples like the rise of Jewish prayer to replace animal sacrifice as a way of worshiping God. This shift didn't happen at once. Prayer was developing as a "disruptive technology" for worshiping God even before the destruction of the Second Temple in 70 CE. The fact that there was no longer a Temple simply helped propel prayer forward. In modern times, musicians like Shlomo Carlebach and Debbie Friedman breathed new life into Jewish prayer by replacing classic *nusach* (Jewish liturgical tunes) with new music that blended traditional words and contemporary melodies.

Chabad has also created a model of disruptive innovation. They are building a platform for Jewish life that exists outside of mainstream Jewish organizations like synagogues and Federations. While a synagogue needs to run full-service operations that include educational, religious, and social programming, as well as pastoral services and building maintenance, Chabad can come into a market and begin working out of homes. The setup costs are lower and the pace of change is faster because there is no existing membership to engage and no lay leadership structure to work through. So while synagogues are implementing "technologies" to sustain themselves, Chabad comes in and has the luxury to function as a "startup" and just focus on disruptive innovation.

Why Innovation Is So Hard for Establishment Organizations

Let's dig a little deeper into why it is so hard for establishment organizations to innovate. There are four dynamics drawn from the business world that have real resonance with some of the challenges we face in the Jewish not-for-profit sector.

Dynamic #1: Resource Dependence

Part of why it is difficult for established organizations to innovate and change is that we already have a large base constituency that we must serve.[7] This base, often called the "core" or, in this book, "Empowerment Jews," tends to control how resources are allocated in well-run organizations.[8] All too often, and despite good intentions, leaders don't realize that when they direct resources to the issues, programs, and experiences that are most relevant to the core, they end up limiting the scope of impact that an organization can have. For example, the more focused the resources become on the priorities of the core group of Empowerment Jews, the harder it becomes to reach Engagement Jews. Jeremy Brochin, the longtime visionary leader of Penn Hillel, used to ask, "Are you spending 75 percent of your time and resources on 25 percent of your constituents?" The purpose of the question was to help leaders see the limitations created by this kind of resource dependence. The only way to truly change and create opportunities for even larger numbers of people to be inspired by Jewish life is to learn how to do two things at once: (1) serve our core constituencies and (2) find ways to seed new and innovative approaches to reach the other groups of Engagement Jews who are not yet connected to Jewish life.

> "Are you spending 75 percent of your time and resources on 25 percent of your constituents?"
> —Jeremy Brochin

Dynamic #2: Innovation Starts Small

New innovations tend to be small in scale and appeal only to relatively limited segments of the population (like the start-up minyan mentioned earlier in this chapter). They are so small, in fact, that most establishment firms have little or no interest in pursuing them because their benefits in the short term will not make a big enough difference in meeting the growth needs of the larger company.

Jewish organizations face the same dynamic. On Penn's campus, this can be seen in the ways in which Hillel and Chabad operate. On a typical Friday night at Penn Hillel, there might be four hundred to five hundred students at different religious services and Shabbat dinners. Once the number of participants is this large, it is very hard to develop new programmatic offerings that will really make a significant difference in the way people experience Shabbat. For example, Penn Hillel might be reluctant to invest significant time and energy to create a new meditation service if only ten students would attend it. In this situation, the additional service only makes a marginal difference in the number of students participating in the Shabbat experience. Therefore, an organization like Penn Hillel might resist making these kinds of innovative changes, so that week to week and year to year, Friday night at Penn Hillel looks pretty much the same. Chabad, however, is in a different strategic position on campus. Their Friday night program is much smaller and more malleable (twenty to thirty students on average). A new program that attracts ten new students would be a significant increase in participation and a worthwhile investment of institutional resources for them. In this way, smaller organizations can be nimble and innovative, because the cost of experimentation and implementation is much lower. In the end, Penn Hillel can sustain its quality programs that reach a large number of students, but Chabad may have a competitive advantage when it comes to innovation and finding the right ways to reach each and every new student they can.

Dynamic #3: New Markets Demand New Technologies

The attributes that make disruptive technologies unattractive in established markets often are the very ones that constitute their greatest value in emerging markets.[9] The needs, preferences, and appetites of the core market are not just different from the fringe markets, they can be diametrically opposed. What this means for the Jewish community is that the very types of Jewish experiences and communities that might be most desired by Empowerment Jews can sometimes be the biggest impediments to reaching new populations of Engagement Jews.

We see a lot of this with respect to the way that people relate to Israel in the Jewish community. Empowerment Jews spend a tremendous amount of time and money on Israel engagement and advocacy, usually focused on the political dimensions of Israel. While the belief that Israel is under attack on campus may occupy a prominent position in the minds of the established Jewish community, it may not feel particularly relevant, for a number of reasons, to Jews who are disconnected from institutional life. First, many Engagement Jews don't even realize that anti-Israel groups are active on campus, because no one in their social circle is an activist on either side of the debate. Second, this group of Jews tends to relate to Israel in more personal or spiritual ways, rather than for political ones.[10] This is just one example that highlights how what might be most important to one group of Jews can be totally irrelevant to another. In order to really innovate and change, an organization has to find ways to appeal to different markets.

Dynamic #4: Innovation Creates a Positive Gravitational Pull

Innovation always seems to shine brightest. Anything that is considered new and cutting edge—even if its impact is relatively small—can attract a lot of attention and inspire a loyal following.

> A particularly visionary philanthropist in New York City gives generously to the UJA-Federation of New York and a huge, successful synagogue in Manhattan. Even though he has many philanthropic interests, he is most excited and passionate about a small start-up minyan that meets every other Friday night and hosts about forty people. While the minyan is really exciting and exceptionally well run, he knows its capacity to make a difference in the lives of Jewish New Yorkers is profoundly dwarfed by the work of the larger Federation and the synagogue. Even with this knowledge, the Jewish start-up occupies a place of prominence in his mind that is totally disproportionate to the work it actually it does.

Why is this philanthropist so excited and focused on the start-up, and less focused on his other charities? While his synagogue and Federation may be successful in reaching huge numbers of people, they do so in ways that are expected and that tend to support the kinds of activities that mainstream Jewish people already do. In contrast, the Jewish start-up he is supporting may reach only a small number of people, but it is totally focused on doing just one thing and doing it really well. Rather than trying to be all things to all people all the time, the start-up has a singular focus and a newness that can inspire donors to become evangelists for it.

This innovation also creates a kind of reverse halo effect that seems to cast the work of the establishment as inherently stale while projecting the work of Jewish start-ups as disproportionally creative and meaningful. When it comes to more established Jewish organizations, even when something new and exciting is actually happening, many people—especially Engagement Jews—tend to assume it is just the same old products dressed up with new marketing. The opposite is true for a start-up. Sometimes a start-up creates an initiative that is not really new or disruptive at all, but because the organization is new, it seems to be totally revolutionary. All of this just makes it harder for establishment organizations to reach new populations, even when they might be doing the right things.

How to Incubate Change from Within

Given how hard it is for organizations to change while continuing to serve their core constituents, what's the way forward? Is there a model for becoming both an establishment organization and a start-up?

In the business world, there seems to be one essential strategy for achieving this goal: continue to run your existing programs while simultaneously creating a separate, autonomous organization charged with building a new and independent set of offerings built on disruptive innovations.[11] Free of the rules, the limits, and the boundaries of the existing organization, this new division can try totally new things, take bigger risks, and develop a plan to reach new markets. Essentially, it can act like a start-up even though it's not.

Take, for example, the two different strategies used by the department stores Woolworth and Dayton Hudson. By the mid-1960s, a few companies were experimenting with a new model of variety store that was built on a discount model (like Walmart) rather than the traditional models of retail.[12] Both Woolworth and Dayton Hudson, who had run successful businesses in the traditional model, now tried to get a foothold in the new discount retail market. Their different strategic approaches led to dramatically different outcomes. Woolworth became the model of what not to do, and Dayton Hudson became the model of how to successfully incubate change from within.

Woolworth launched Woolco in 1962 and kept the new stores close to its existing core business. The new stores were forced to play by the same rules as the traditional business. They even had the same managers.[13] While the leadership was willing to try something new, they didn't want the new enterprise to cut into the core business of traditional Woolworth stores.[14] In the end, nothing really changed. Woolco wasn't given the freedom to grow and

> "Everything in this world can be imitated except for the truth, because an artificial, counterfeit truth is not the truth at all."
>
> —Rabbi Menachem Mendel of Kotzk

compete in the new market, and the same factors that prevented Woolworth from winning in the discount retail space also prevented Woolco from succeeding. By 1982, Woolco failed. By 1997, the final remaining Woolworth store closed its doors, and the once-dominant retail chain was overtaken by newer, faster companies like Walmart.

Meanwhile, the Dayton Hudson Corporation took a different approach. Rather than starting a new division and then trying to control it, they created a totally new store built on the discount model in a suburb outside of Saint Paul, Minnesota. This store was the prototype of today's Target stores. Target was allowed to grow and develop on its own. It was allowed to create its own brand and its own corporate culture. Target hired its own management team, and empowered them to create a new set of metrics and practices that were best suited for their particular business model. The Dayton Hudson Corporation even went so far as to let Target compete against the other Dayton Hudson brands. In the end, Target was so successful that Dayton Hudson sold the department store side of their business to Marshall Field in 1999 and changed the corporate name to Target in 2000. Target's current annual revenues are over $72 million.[15]

"Ready, Fire, Aim": Making Real Choices

If Jewish organizations want to change, they need to do so in bold and dramatic ways. The only way for well-established organizations to innovate is to make real choices—to set aside significant resources (both human and financial) and grant new people the power to try out their ideas, even if the leadership does not fully understand these ideas or know if they will work. Rabbi Rick Jacobs, president of the Union for Reform Judaism,

"Our Rabbis taught: Once Rosh Hashanah fell on Shabbat [and all the cities were gathering together]. Rabban Yohanan ben Zakkai said to the Bathyrians—"Let's blow shofar!" They said to him: "Let's discuss." He said to them, "Let's blow shofar first, and then we'll discuss." After they blew, they said to him, "Let's discuss!" He said to them: "The horn has already been sounded in Yavneh, and we don't reverse after the deed is done."
—Talmud, *Rosh HaShanah* 29b

speaking to a group of rabbis in Philadelphia, said that the need for change is so critical that we do not have time for a lot of process—we need to try out new models for change even if we're not sure they will work. So rather than taking a "ready, aim, fire" approach, it's time for a "ready, fire, aim" approach. In the next chapter, we will look at a real-life example from Penn Hillel of how the theory of disruptive innovation can spark new innovation in an existing Jewish organization.

Questions for Further Consideration

1. Does your organization spend 75 percent of its time and money on 25 percent of your constituents? If not, what do you think the percentages really are?

2. How do you define constituents? Is it by who participates? Who is a member? Who donates? Does it include Jewish and non-Jewish family members? Does it include extended family members beyond parents and children?

3. What would it look like if your organization dramatically expanded its definition of constituents to include any Jewish person who is within your sphere of influence?

4. What kind of time, money, staff, or volunteer leadership would you need in order to engage people within that large definition?

5. What are the ways that your organization encourages innovation? What are the ways that it stifles it?

4

Disruptive Innovation at Penn Hillel

It's Friday night, and somewhere off campus a young rabbi with a beard and tattoos on his forearms walks into one of the fraternity houses. The guys have already starting drinking a bit, and they are all ready to sit down to Shabbat dinner. After all the food is served, the rabbi begins to facilitate a conversation about the "Torah of hooking up in college." Even though Hillel bought the food and pays the salary of the rabbi, nothing about the event feels like Hillel. There is no logo. There was no banner on campus advertising the event. It's not even a program. It's just a bunch of fraternity guys getting together to have Shabbat dinner on their own terms and to hang out with a rabbi they know really gets them. For many of them, it's the first time they've ever been part of a Shabbat dinner that wasn't hosted by their parents or grandparents. Something about it feels different from other Jewish experiences they've had. They didn't have to leave their regular lives and friends to go somewhere else to "do Jewish." It's the first time that their Jewish lives and their fraternity lives feel integrated. It's also the first time for many of them to have a conversation with a rabbi who came to meet them on their own turf. It's not in a synagogue or connected to a life-cycle event. It's in the basement of a grimy and beer-soaked fraternity house.

This Shabbat dinner isn't the only one happening outside of Hillel that night. There are more than a dozen student interns also hosting Shabbat dinners of their own all over campus.

Just as important as the informal gatherings taking place off campus, there are also three different Shabbat dinners taking place in the Hillel building that night. The dining hall is full of the usual suspects. On the second floor, the Reform Jewish Community is having their own Shabbat dinner, with a discussion about which prayers were removed from the Reform siddur and why. On the third floor, the Orthodox Community at Penn is hosting another dinner with a scholar-in-residence from a yeshiva in Israel.

What I just described is not what people typically think of when they imagine Hillel Shabbat dinners. So how did the model of Shabbat dinner at Hillel grow from a staff-run program in the building for a relatively small number of regulars to a model where dozens of students are each hosting their own Shabbat dinners all over campus, each with a different group of friends, each with a different brand, and each with a different feel?

It took Penn Hillel decades to evolve to this point, and I want to share with you everything we've learned along the way. Today, Penn Hillel runs two different operating systems for Jewish life at the same time. In the building, under the banner of Hillel, we specialize in working with Empowerment students with stronger Jewish backgrounds. Outside the building, we run the Jewish Renaissance Project (JRP), which is finely tuned to reach over 1,300 Engagement students each year. We often say that Hillel is the best version of an establishment Jewish organization—like many of the best synagogues, Federations, and JCCs around the country—while JRP is like a Jewish start-up that can operate on the fringe.

As I tell you this story, I hope it will resonate with some of the same challenges and questions you are struggling with in your own organization. Of course, there are real differences between the work that Hillel does with college students and the work that synagogues, JCCs, and Federations do with Jewish adults. And yet, I believe that we can learn from one another. I offer the Hillel model not as the solution for your organization's particular set of challenges, but rather as a prompt to get you thinking in new ways. Each organization is different, and each group of leaders will need to find the right ways to adapt and translate this model to their own situation.

What Led to the Creation of the Jewish Renaissance Project?

Much like other well-established Jewish organizations, Penn Hillel had become a victim of its own success. With the nearly three hundred events per month, five hundred student participants a week, and over a thousand different students engaged each year, Penn Hillel's institutional resources were stretched to the limit with their core programmatic offerings alone. Even though the staff and student leadership were deeply committed to reaching every Jew on campus, Hillel just didn't have the capacity to reach new students.

I remember my first High Holy Day season working at Penn Hillel. We ran several huge services filled with three thousand students and community members. It was only when I walked outside the auditorium and began to make my way across campus that I realized something: while we were busy running services for a huge number of students, other campus Jewish groups were out there building relationships with students, offering learner services, and hosting small and intimate holiday meals. It's not that Hillel didn't want to be doing this smaller, more relational work; it was just that we were already too busy just running services. Beyond High Holy Day services, we had to run Mitzvah Day, Israel week, kosher dining, and weekly Shabbat services for Reform, Conservative, and Orthodox students. While each of these responsibilities was important, they tended to attract the same types of students over and over again, and we had little time or money left over to help us reach new people. Our Hillel was full, yet we weren't fulfilling our mission. I remember feeling like I had to spend all of my time with students discussing program logistics, budgets, and publicity, when what I really wanted to do was discuss how Judaism could help them answer the biggest questions they were facing at this transformative time in their lives. All of the clutter of the constant programming prevented us from being able to do the real work of helping to inspire students to grow into Jewish adulthood.

As I tell this story, my guess is that you may see the same challenges in your own organization. Think of a local pulpit rabbi you know. By the time he or she finishes all the meetings, officiates at the funerals, weddings, and *b'nei mitzvah*, attends to pastoral care, and leads regular prayer services, there is literally no time left for other work that might help engage new people.

This kind of situation has a real impact on people's lives:

> A recent Penn graduate named Sam was living in a large Midwestern city. He had just started his own business and was on the precipice of making a lot of money, something he had never intended to do in his life. In response to his concerns about how wealth might negatively affect who he was and how he understood his life, he reached out to me for help in finding a local rabbi with whom to study Torah. I connected him with many fantastic Reform and Conservative rabbis in his city, and each of them responded in more or less the same way. They offered him membership brochures, information about adult education classes, a list of books to read on his own, and programmatic offerings from the men's club that had nothing to do with Torah learning. Sam wasn't looking to join an institution; he was looking for a relationship. In the end, Sam did find someone to learn with him. A local Orthodox outreach rabbi from Aish HaTorah was willing to come to his office and learn with him each week. While he liked the rabbi, the learning did not really fit his needs, but he kept doing it because this rabbi was the only one available.

What a missed opportunity for Sam and for the denominational synagogues in town! The problem in this story is not the rabbis or the organizations they work for. The problem is that they rely on a broken model. These institutions require so much time and money to sustain themselves that they never have the bandwidth to innovate or to reach new types of Jews. By contrast, the Aish HaTorah rabbi, while also very busy, does not have the institutional responsibilities that fill the other rabbis' schedules. This makes it easier and far more likely that he will be able to be highly responsive to a Jewish individual who wants to learn.

Turning the Corner: Five Rules for Applying Disruptive Innovation

Over the years and through many innovative attempts (both failed and successful), Penn Hillel, in creating and building JRP, has developed five rules for how to build a model of disruptive innovation from within our own organization.

Rule #1: The Rule of *Tzimtzum*

The good news at Penn Hillel was that we had great participation numbers at most of our initiatives. The bad news was that once those events and spaces were full of regulars, it was always hard to welcome new people— especially if they had a different Jewish story from the regulars. So the question became "How do you make room when there is no room?" For years, we thought the answer was to try to attract new people by offering great new initiatives that were marketed especially for new students. But that never really worked.

Each time Penn Hillel created an innovative new set of events, the "regulars" would sign up and fill the slots before new students could even show up. These Empowerment Jews had a competitive advantage—they tended to be more Jewishly confident and self-motivated, so of course they would jump at the chance participate in something new and exciting. The problem was that once the initiative was even partially filled by the regulars, it was no longer a new and safe space for Engagement Jews. Regardless of the activity or the marketing, this new space ended up looking and feeling just like all the other Hillel programs on campus. This meant that when new students showed up at an event, even though it was marketed for them, they often ended up feeling out of place.

We overcame this dynamic by employing what we call the rule of *tzimtzum*. The concept of *tzimtzum* is that before God could create the world, God needed to contract, to shrink God's self in order to make room for something new. This contraction is known in Jewish tradition as *tzimtzum*. This principle can also be applied to organizations that want to develop new ways of reaching different Jewish populations. Real engagement cannot just be about funneling more people into the same programmatic offerings. An organization needs to create new and open spaces that are intentionally designed to meet the needs of Engagement Jews. For example, while

"When it arose in God's will to create, God contracted [*tzimtzum* in Hebrew] God's self into one small point at the center, in order to allow for enough space for creation."

—Adapted from Rabbi Isaac Luria

it might be intimidating to come to Hillel to join a discussion hosted by one of the existing pro-Israel groups, it might not be as intimidating to show up at a brunch at your friend's house to have the same discussion. By taking what is essentially the same conversation out of the institutional setting and re-creating it in an organic and informal place, everything changes. So many of the social dynamics and barriers to involvement that plague large programmatic offerings disappear. This new space has the capacity to help an organization not only increase the numbers of Jews it reaches but also to increase the diversity of those Jews.

Rule #2: Avoiding the Bait-and-Switch Dynamic of Outreach

Another problematic dynamic we were trying to avoid in the creation of the Jewish Renaissance Project (JRP) was the bait-and-switch dynamic that was present in older outreach models.[1] Some Hillels would have their younger "cool" staff go out to campus to have coffee with students or plan light and fun social programs that would attract new people. While the stated goal was to bring Jewish life to campus, there was always an ulterior motive of trying to use these coffee dates and social programs as a way of getting more Engagement Jews to come to Hillel. Students could always sense this coming, and often the Hillel representatives really struggled with imposing this agenda.

"No purpose intervenes between I and You, no greed and no anticipation... Every means is an obstacle. Only where all means have disintegrated encounters occur."

—Martin Buber

Nearly a decade ago, when Penn Hillel was re-creating JRP, the goal was to do something different. The real mission of Hillel was never to get people "involved" in Hillel; it was always to create the relationships, experiences, and communities that provoked students to engage in a process of "Jewish self-authorship." Hillel's real goal, in other words, was to help Jews grow into fully self-actualized Jewish adults.[2] If the goal was really about Jewish growth, then it didn't matter whether students "got involved" or "showed up"; it only mattered if we could help create powerful opportunities for Jewish growth. This shift freed Penn Hillel from the need to recruit students to fill the existing programs and build a stronger relationship with Jewish organizations. Instead, it allowed us to focus on the student's relationship with Judaism.

Rule #3: Half Measures and the Rule of Epidemics

Over the years, Hillel has tried many different approaches to "get new people involved." This generally took the form of new programming, with "sexy" promotional materials and giveaways. But these initiatives usually took up a lot of staff time and cost a lot of money without actually attracting many new people. In many ways, each of these attempts was a kind of half measure in trying to rebrand Hillel or engage new students.[3] At their very core, these programs were really just the same old events, run by the same staff, with the same student leaders, dressed up with hipper marketing.

My mentor, Jeremy Brochin, found a way to overcome this challenge by using some of the ideas in Malcolm Gladwell's book *The Tipping Point*. In particular, Jeremy focused on the importance of Gladwell's idea of the "rule of epidemics." While we often think that change comes in incremental steps after long periods of hard work, real change takes place quite rapidly and in quantum leaps.[4] A great example of this was the meteoric rise in popularity of Hush Puppies shoes. In the early 1990s, sales for the classic American brushed-suede shoes were down to 30,000 pairs annually. But somehow in the mid-1990s the shoes became "cool." In 1995, the company sold 430,000 pairs of shoes. The following year, they sold four times that number.[5] In this case, the change was quick and dramatic.

Something about this phenomenon rang true for Penn Hillel and other Jewish organizations. If we wanted to really make a change in the way we reached Engagement Jews, we would have to do something *big*, and something that avoided the pitfalls of incremental change.

Rule #4: The Rule of Bifurcation

To achieve the kind of transformative change we were looking for and to avoid all of the pitfalls that hampered previous attempts at innovation,

Penn Hillel adopted a rule of bifurcation that was similar to the approach that Dayton Hudson took with its Target stores. When JRP launched, it was created to be separate and distinct from Penn Hillel. It had its own brand, its own website, its own set of initiatives, and its own staff and funders.

Bifurcation of the staff was the most important step. JRP staff didn't have any responsibilities to be in the Hillel building for events, to get to know the existing student leaders, or to help coach any of the existing student groups. The only way for us to really network and meet the hundreds of students who were not already engaged in Jewish life on campus was to hire new staff who had the time, skills, and personal narrative necessary to do it. The JRP staff had no office. They were deployed to different places on campus. They worked in the student union, the freshman quad, even the library—anywhere outside of the Hillel building. The goal was that JRP staff should work in the same places where students lived, worked, and played, and be totally focused on the students who were not already connected. Freed from all of the institutional responsibilities, they could be fully devoted to building relationships with Engagement Jews and helping them grow in their Judaism without the need to drive attendance to existing programming.

JRP staff had simple and focused job descriptions: build relationships with 180 students who are not already engaged in Jewish campus life and be entrepreneurial in creating news ways to reach them.[6] Everything was fair game. Shabbat dinners, new social justice projects, Jewish learning, and alternative expressions of Jewish prayer were all options. It was even okay if the Jewish engagement didn't lead to any kind of programmatic activity at all. As long as there was significant Jewish content present in their conversations, relationship building alone was enough to make a big impact on the student's Jewish growth.[7]

As you can imagine, in the early years, this open-ended mission was a bit unwieldy, and it left the JRP staff to reinvent the wheel every semester or at least every year. In time, the model became more solid and fixed without losing its ability to be highly customizable based on the students with whom our staff was meeting.

Rule #5: Running Two Different Operating Systems at the Same Time

The launch of JRP was about more than just bifurcation of staff responsibilities. Penn Hillel needed two operating systems for Jewish life, each with a separate brand. We thought of this in part like the Gap/Old Navy/Banana Republic trio—three brands in the same company that each appeal to a different market. No matter how nice the clothes are at Old Navy, some people will still prefer to shop at Banana Republic. Why would people relate any differently to Jewish organizations?

Hillel's core program's mission is to serve as many Jews as possible in the deepest way possible while still operating in the conventional Jewish community model—a vertical leadership structure with a formal division between leaders and participants. The JRP model, however, seeks to reach Jews who are not already connected to a Hillel initiative or who do not feel comfortable in institutional Jewish spaces. JRP is totally horizontal in a way that minimizes the distinction between leaders and participants and minimizes any kind of social, geographical, or educational barriers to involvement in Jewish life. While students come to Hillel to explore Judaism, JRP goes out and brings Jewish life to students wherever they are.

> "Why did God divide up Israel by tribe and not give the inheritance to all of Israel? Every nation is blessed with unique national traits. Each nation possesses special talents and makes a unique contribution to the world. This specialty may lie in the arts, sciences, organizational ability..."
> —Adapted from Rav Kook

We also made the difficult decision that we were not going to be concerned with competition between JRP and Hillel's core programs. We wanted both to succeed, and in order to do that we had to give each of them the room necessary to grow and develop independently. If JRP wanted to have a presence during new student orientation, a prime time for Hillel to connect with freshmen, they were allowed. If JRP wanted to plan a major event at the same time as a Hillel event, no one stopped them. As you can imagine, there were times when staff or student leaders felt a sense of competition or redundancy. And yet, we continue to allow this overlap even today because of the belief that if Hillel and JRP are really doing what they are designed to, there will ultimately be no conflict; each event will be engaging different types of students. One of the foundational ideas that informs this methodology is that there is no single event that is right for everyone and for every different type of Jewish intelligence. With the wide range of potential participants in mind, the theory is that a more robust and diverse set of events, as long as they are deployed to different populations, only increase our chances for reaching more Jewish students.

Managing the of Politics of Disruptive Innovation

You may be wondering how we managed the politics of creating this new sub-organization with our existing stakeholders. The truth is, student and volunteer leaders were surprisingly open to this idea because there was such a need for a new way of reaching students. Over the years, the initial tensions and politics that arose at the creation of JRP have faded, and we have been able to effect a culture change so that both student leaders in the core program and longtime Penn Hillel supporters see the benefits of running two different operating systems, and are even proud of it.

That said, the following are some of the key ways that we framed the conversation with existing student leaders in order to minimize any damaging political fallout from these changes:

- The Hillel core programs and their student leaders were already pushed to the max just trying to maintain the programs that reached approximately one thousand of the twenty-five hundred Jewish undergraduate students at Penn. Asking the same leaders to do more simply was not a possibility. Therefore, the creation of JRP felt like it was a win-win solution to a shared problem.
- While there was going to be a bifurcation of the staff, there would be no prior bifurcation of students. The mission of Hillel's core program was still to try to reach every single Jewish student on campus. JRP would step in only to help engage the students who fell through the cracks. This helped minimize the feelings of territorial control that Hillel core leaders might have.
- JRP was funded by new money, often coming from new donors. This ensured that the new initiative did not cannibalize the resources necessary for the core programs.

- Finally, we tried to make sure that JRP was not overly visible in the Hillel building, in order to minimize opportunities for friction. JRP events and promotional materials were all located outside of the building. JRP was left to be a quiet little start-up that operated in other spaces and with populations of students where Hillel had not yet succeeded.

While the politics of creating change are certainly different in each organization, I want to show you how it was done at Penn Hillel as a way of encouraging other organizational leaders not to refrain from innovation simply because of fears of political fallout. With the combination of the right idea and the right communication strategy, it can be done!

What JRP Really Looks Like on the Ground

While the methodology has continued to develop and be refined, JRP and Hillel's core programs still look basically as they are described above. Penn Hillel still runs two different operating systems, under two different brands, with two different staffs.

The only major difference from the original JRP model is that it has grown dramatically in both number and depth:

- Today, in addition to the 1,000 students reached by Hillel's core program, JRP engages an additional 1,300 students each year.
- While the Hillel core programs support about twenty-four student groups and approximately 250 student leadership positions, JRP now has an additional eleven initiatives that create new leadership opportunities for an average of 160 students each year, many of whom are student interns.
- Most of the interns participate in weekly small group sessions that are heavily focused on a particular form of Jewish learning (see chapter 7 about educational philosophy) and leadership development in something we call peer-to-peer engagement (see chapter 9 for a more in-depth look at this methodology).

The different JRP initiatives have been developed in very careful and strategic ways. In the early years, staff were constantly reinventing the wheel, which was unsustainable and even counterproductive. Therefore, in order to create some sustainable structures, JRP staff began to analyze the information gathered through the thousands of coffee dates and one-on-one conversations with Engagement Jews. The same kinds of issues and desires seemed to keep coming up over and over again. JRP staff used this data to build initiatives that could bring together groups of students who were struggling with the same types of things. More than that, each initiative was designed in a way that the structure stayed the same year-to-year, while the specific content of the Jewish learning and the types of student-run events could change based on each new group of students. We joked about this and called it "institutionalizing innovation." It was our way of building enough structure that we could meet the expectations of our donors, while ensuring that JRP could remain a highly adaptable and cutting-edge way of engaging Jewish students.

In practical terms, this meant that each year there were specialized student internship programs for freshmen in the Quad, sophomores in the Greek system, juniors and seniors living off campus, and Birthright Israel alumni. Each of these initiatives had general metrics for both depth and breadth goals, yet the specifics of the Jewish learning and the kinds of events that student interns created were tied to the needs and interests of each unique group. In this way, the staff could still meet JRP's benchmarks of success each year without having to lose the "start-up" feel or the students' ability to be co-creators in the experience.

As JRP began to grow and become more established, we were concerned that it would lose its innovation culture and begin to fall into many of the same traps that establishment organizations do. There were two main strategic concerns: follow-through with alumni of JRP student internships and keeping JRP internships designated for Engagement Jews only.

Follow-Through with Alumni of JRP Internships

As JRP grew, the question of how to follow through with student interns after their first year of engagement became a real concern. While the staff wanted to continue to invest in each of these students, we did not want them to take away entry-level spots from new Engagement Jews. Additionally, we didn't want to force them into the Hillel infrastructure if it could not provide them with the appropriate next step in their Jewish journey.

In order to address these issues, JRP staff created something called JRP2, which became the umbrella initiative for how to engage students after their first year with JRP. The key elements of the JRP2 program are as follows:

- Set aside significant staff time and financial resources to continue to engage former JRP student interns.
- Create optional passageways for students who are interested and ready to get more connected to Hillel core programs. Each year, about 30 percent of JRP1 alumni become active in existing Hillel initiatives.
- Create a next set of opp ortunities for Jewish learning and growth. Today we call this JRP Lab, and it often takes the form of a weekly learning community with a much deeper intellectual focus and more intensive text study.
- Set aside money to help support JRP1 alumni who are interested in becoming Jewish "entrepreneurs" and in creating new initiatives.

Keeping JRP Internships for Engagement Students

In terms of keeping JRP programs focused on reaching students far outside of the organized Jewish community, JRP staff created an internal set of benchmarks to guide the recruitment process of student interns. We have managed to maintain roughly the following breakdown over the years:

- Twenty percent of the students have never been institutionally connected to Judaism. These are the students who did not have a bar or bat mitzvah ceremony, whose families did not belong to synagogues, or who did not participate in a Passover seder or Hanukkah candle lighting on an annual basis.[8]
- Sixty percent of the students have some level of past affiliation (for example, they did have a bar or bat mitzvah ceremony) but have not participated in organized Jewish life since then.
- Twenty percent of the students have higher levels of past affiliation, meaning they may have participated in some kind of Jewish camp or youth group growing up, but have not yet been engaged in campus Jewish life.

Since the creation of these metrics, JRP staff has been able to ensure that these student internships do not end up being filled by students who could have just as easily been leaders in Hillel's core programs.

In addition to these measures of past Jewish involvement, JRP has additional criteria for the ideal JRP intern. They need to be social connectors, mavens, and "salesmen"[9] who operate in social networks with a lot of Jews who are not yet engaged by Hillel's core programs. This could mean, for example, students who were leaders in the fraternity or sorority system, student government, or the performing arts community.

Financial Concerns and Some Surprising Positive Outcomes

When I am presenting these ideas at a conference or organizational board retreat, it's at this point that someone asks, "While all of these ideas sound nice, how can we possibly pay for programs like this when our budget is already so tight?" The truth is that it doesn't have to cost a lot of money to start some kind of engagement initiative. There are many small Hillels around the country with limited budgets that have launched some version of the JRP program with only a few thousand dollars. But there is another point that is equally important. While it tends to be hard to raise money to sustain an organization, it can be relatively easy to raise new funds for something innovative and transformative!

Today, Penn Hillel raises $500,000 a year for JRP in addition to our annual fundraising that supports our core programs. There have been many donors who were reluctant to support Hillel but who are now excited to support JRP, because it's different and because the idea of engaging students outside of the building resonates with their own Jewish experience. More than that, some of the donors who get engaged through JRP also end up supporting Hillel more broadly.

In this way, a virtuous cycle is created. Because Penn Hillel is seen as an innovator and thought leader, we are more successful in attracting funders to support our work. The better funded we are, the more successful we are at engaging more students in more meaningful ways, which in turn leads to more successful fund-raising. I point this out not to brag but only to make an important point: success breeds success. The only way for an organization that feels stuck to move forward is by taking a risk and trying to do something that can be transformative for people. While no strategy or programmatic offering can solve all of the problems of the Jewish community, creative and visionary innovation can help change the story of your organization and create a kind of positive momentum that can help usher in a new period of growth and reinvention.

> "When a person feels joy while performing the mitzvah, that person is immediately rewarded with more joy."
> —Rabbi Yaakov Culi

Applying the JRP and Penn Hillel Model to Other Organizations

Ultimately the question of how to apply this model to other organizations is one that will be answered by the creative and visionary professionals and volunteer leaders from that organization. That said, here are five principles that can help:

1. **Make real choices about allocating time and resources.** The only way to truly foster change is to commit real time and money to these projects. For larger organizations, this might mean reprioritizing staff time and existing discretionary budgets. For smaller organizations with limited staff and budgets, this might mean using the opportunity to launch a new initiative as a chance to begin a new kind of fundraising.

2. **Diversity breeds diversity.** To reach different types of Jews, an organization needs to hire different types of staff people. For Engagement Jews, this means hiring staff who share the same background as the people you are trying to reach. At Penn Hillel, we have found that the most effective engagement professionals tend to have similar Jewish stories: they grew up disconnected from organized Jewish life but were turned on later in life by a special person or experience that really changed the way they think about Judaism.[10] An additional benefit of hiring staff who don't fit the mold is that they can also challenge many of the assumptions about Jewish life that other professional and lay leaders in the organization have internalized.

3. **Move from program planning to relationship building.** The first thing we put in every JRP job description now is "build relationships with 180 students who are not already connected to Jewish life." Relationships are everything. The only way for staff to make a transformative difference in the lives of Engagement Jews is to cultivate a large number of deep, personal relationships.

4. **The experience is more important than the brand.** Early on in JRP, we decided that creating deep, intimate, and challenging Jewish experiences was much more important than getting people to feel loyal to our brand. There are thousands of students who have been impacted by JRP and Hillel without ever knowing it. We heard it countless times from students: "I've never done anything with Hillel, but I am going to Josh's house tonight for Shabbat dinner." Even though that student doesn't know that the dinner was sponsored by JRP, we see it as a success.

5. **The best way to secure the institution is to forget about the institution.** If your organization can focus on innovation and impacting people's Jewish lives, people will be attracted to it—not because you recruited them or solicited them, but because people want to be associated with and invested in organizations that inspire them and make a difference in their lives.

What the JRP Model Might Look Like in an Adult Community

Creating JRP was never a binary choice between in-reach and outreach—the goal was always to continue supporting the Hillel model while simultaneously incubating a model of disruptive innovation on the side. Even though the Hillel core programs were strong and successful, it was often hard for Engagement Jews to find their way in. So we recognized that the only way to meet the needs of both the Empowerment Jews and the Engagement Jews was to run two different operating systems for Jewish life. Each one could be perfectly calibrated for the distinct interests, needs, and Jewish backgrounds of these different populations. Nearly a decade into this most recent iteration of JRP, Hillel is stronger now than ever and JRP is reaching students far outside of the Hillel core. Interestingly, in recent years, Hillel core student leaders and staff are starting to see JRP as a learning lab for their own approach to Jewish life. They are constantly looking to see how and where the best JRP strategies from outside the building can be incorporated into the core programs happening inside the building.

Now that we have taken a deep dive into how these methodologies are applied on campus, let's imagine for a moment what it might look like if they were applied to an adult Jewish community. Let's take, for example, a synagogue that is trying to engage more people to participate in a Sunday morning Torah study class taught by the rabbi. Currently the class is attended by thirty people each week. In the classic model of a Jewish organization, the leadership would develop better publicity, promote it on social media, offer better food, and talk it up among their friends. If these tactics work, the class might double in size to sixty people a week. This is great and exactly what they should do; but it's only the first step.

In addition to doubling the number of people coming to the Torah study class, the JRP model would then suggest that the staff go out and recruit fifteen additional people who are not part of the class and don't normally come to synagogue learning programs to be part of a *new* fellowship. Ideally, these fellows would also represent different social networks around the city and have lots of social connections with other Engagement Jews. The fellows would meet on a weekly or monthly basis. The rabbi and the synagogue would make a major investment in their Jewish lives and leadership skills. Eventually, the fellows could meet with the rabbi on Tuesday night to learn about the weekly Torah portion, and then each of them could host their own Torah study brunch at their house on Sunday morning. Even if each class were small—only ten people—there would be another 150 people studying Torah in addition to the sixty new people already connected to the standing Torah study class. By empowering the fellows to create their own Torah discussion, not only does the synagogue increase its numbers, but also by increasing the number and diversity of the type of Jews who lead Torah study, each class hosted by a different fellow will inevitably play to different types of Jewish intelligences. The rabbi could lead professional-style Jewish learning based on his or her set of skills and abilities, and peer leaders could lead additional kinds of Jewish learning that would be particular to their own Jewish perspective and those of their social network. In the end, having many different people teach dramatically increases the diversity of ways to access Jewish learning. The synagogue could then also take steps to weave these different networks of people together. Perhaps the rabbi shows up at different people's houses to teach a few times a year so these external networks get to know the rabbi. Perhaps there is a huge Shabbat dinner once or twice a year to honor everyone who's participated so that everyone can see that they are part of something larger than just their small learning group.

This is just one example, and it's just intended to get you thinking about how this could work for your organization, be it a Hillel, a JCC, a Federation, or a synagogue.

Questions for Further Consideration

1. While an internship works for college students, what form would this need to take to work with adults? Could a fellowship or an ambassador model work?

2. On campus, we pay student interns four hundred dollars a year. What kind of incentives would be necessary for adults?

3. In JRP, we run different fellowships for different groups of people (such as freshmen, Greek students, and upperclassmen). What would the different groups be for your organization? What are the natural target populations and social networks that are reachable for your organization?

4. If your organization wanted to create something like JRP for adults, who would object? What fears and concerns would motivate their objections?

5. What nontraditional funding sources could you find to create a model of disruptive innovation for your organization? Are their people, foundations, or partners who might not support your organization under normal circumstances but who might for something really innovative?

6. In Hillel, we invest in these cohort groups, and then they graduate and leave campus. In adult Jewish organizations, people are

less transient. Imagine if you had fifteen fellows each year over the course of five to ten years who were all still connected in some way to your organization. When you look five to ten years into the future, how can you imagine making use of the network of former fellows to help transform your organization?

5

Moving from Clubs to Networks

New Ways of Understanding Community

Do you ever find yourself sitting at some kind of meeting for the Jewish community and it just hits you that the organization is stuck? No matter what the agenda of the meeting is, the conversation always seems to go back to the same kind of questions that focus on how the organization can better motivate people to do the things that it needs them to do so that it can be stronger and healthier. If these are the kinds of questions that you or your organization tend to focus on, you may be stuck in the Club Model of Jewish community:

- Do you find that you or your organization is really focused on how to attract new members or how to get more people to show up at your building or programs?
- Do you ever find yourself thinking something like, "We have a great product, and our work is important; if people just knew about it and could experience it, they would love it too"?
- Have you tried many different ways to make your organization more warm and welcoming to newcomers, only to find that it

doesn't work? After a few months, do people revert to their old habits of being cliquey or insular, or do you find that it doesn't really matter because there aren't enough newcomers for all of that work to make a real difference?

- Do you ever find yourself or your organization responding to people who are doing Jewish things outside of an institutional context as if they are a problem? For example, "Wouldn't it be better for all of those new independent giving circles to just give their money directly to Federation?" Or "Is the reason that synagogue programs are suffering from low attendance due to the fact that so many families are hosting their own Shabbat dinners rather than coming to the official ones sponsored by the synagogue?"

For years, Penn Hillel was stuck too. It seemed like no matter what we did, both the leaders in the building and the disconnected people outside the building were not interested in change. They all just assumed that Hillel's mission was limited to getting people to show up for Shabbat dinner and services. Even when we tried to change and find new ways to diversify the types of programs we offered and the types of students who showed up, it never seemed to make a difference. Each year, we asked the same questions, and each year we came up with more or less the same answers, which led to the same kind of limited success.

So how did we turn the corner and free ourselves from the Club Model? Of course, there isn't one single answer to that question, but there is a set of tools that really helped, and I want to share them with you now. They were developed as training tools for the JCSC Fellowship. The thinking was that if JCSC fellows were being hired to do a new kind of work, then they would need a new kind of training that could help them imagine new ways of thinking about Jewish community.[1]

As we proceed, imagine that we are looking at and analyzing these different diagrams together. Over the years, I have found that these images make great tools for training both professional and volunteer leaders. I hope the diagrams help provoke a new conversation about the role that organizations have in creating community and how they help foster Jewish life. Additionally, sharing these three models will help us process and synthesize some of the ideas and methodologies laid out in the previous chapters.

Model #1: The Club Model

Examine figure 1 and take note of what it teaches us about how community functions. As you look at it, please consider the following questions:

1. What are the differences between the people on the inside of the box and the people on the outside?
2. What do you think the arrows and the box represent, and what do they communicate about how the Club Model functions?
3. Where is Judaism present, and where is it not?

One of the first features that people immediately notice about this model is that the people outside of the box are individuals who look different from one another, but the people inside the box all look the same. They are all generic gray figures without any individual identity other than the Jewish star that defines them. Whoever they really are, they appear in this image to be nothing more than Jewish clones who are all part of one shared "community." While all clubs and communities have internal diversity, the point of this diagram is to highlight how it feels to the outsider when

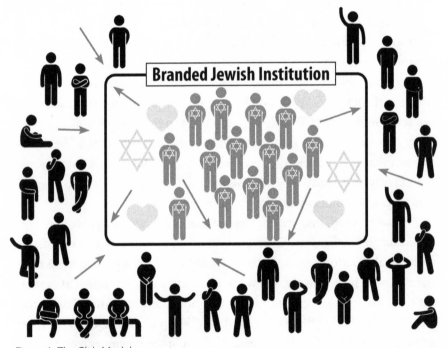

Branded Jewish Institution

Figure 1. The Club Model

he perceives that everyone on the inside is the same. This is, of course, a common dynamic in the organized Jewish world.

> It's the first Shabbat dinner of the year. Hillel is packed with first-year students, who all look nervous and out of place. By the end of the first month of school, they will all look like they own the place, but tonight they still hold themselves like high school students. The Hillel rabbi walks up to a group of freshmen huddled together to introduce herself. She can read that they are nervous, so she asks, "How does this scene strike you? There are a lot of Jews here, right?" By asking the question, she names the exact thing the students are feeling and gives them permission to open up. The first thing they say is that it seems like everyone knows everyone else already. In making that observation, one of the student points to a group of students all standing together across the lobby. What the rabbi knows that the students don't is that she has just come from talking to that group of students. They are also freshmen. They also feel overwhelmed and intimidated. In fact, they just said the same thing to her and pointed to the group of students she is now talking to as proof that everyone knows everyone else.

One of the great challenges created by macro-community gatherings where the Club Model is in effect is that in a whole room of new people, everyone assumes that he or she must be on the outside of that box, while "those people over there" are on the inside. The students all project their own fears and insecurities on others. This happens all the time in Jewish community situations. At a Federation event, a new person assumes that everyone is rich or that everyone has one set of political views on Israel, when in fact the room is filled with diverse types of Jews. Alternatively, at a synagogue, a new person may assume that everyone is more religious or knowledgeable than she is, even though many other people are feeling the same way.

> "And Moses answered and said: 'But, behold, they will not believe me, nor listen to my voice; for they will say: The Lord has not appeared to you.'"
> —Exodus 4:1

Sometimes this is just a projection, and other times it is real. Institutions that operate as clubs do have certain norms that prevent newcomers from feeling welcome. These are also the same norms that help people on the inside feel like they are a part of something special. So while the Club Model really works for those on the inside, it doesn't always work for newcomers, especially if they are post-institutional in their orientation. The feeling of being different or of being an outsider can lead them to adopt a more generalized belief that all Jewish institutions are "bland, conformist, conservative, judgmental, and laden with an 'agenda' of one sort or another."[2] A common critique of Jewish institutions from outsiders is that all of the regulars seem to be the same and that they all fit into conventional categories—everyone seems to be married with kids.[3] Everyone seems to be heterosexual and working in white-collar jobs as doctors, lawyers, and businesspeople. I had friends who moved to a new city and tried to get hooked in to the Jewish community. As they struggled to get integrated, their joke became "We are just one kid short of a great social life."

> "Just as we accept that our neighbor's face does not resemble ours, so must we accept that our neighbor's views do not resemble ours."
> —Rabbi Menachem Mendel of Kotzk

A second feature of the diagram that you will notice is the impermeable box that separates those on the outside from those on the inside. This boundary can take many forms. It can be dues, membership, or the location of the physical building. Other boundaries include Jewish knowledge, socioeconomic level, age, and even marital status. It is anything that creates or reinforces a sense that there are barriers to involvement or that certain conditions need to be met in order to be part of a community.

Also notice that in the Club Model, Judaism exists in the box, representing spaces that are specifically and formally Jewish. This means that if and when you want to do something Jewish, you need to leave your "normal life" and show up at an official Jewish space. A core belief in doing engagement work is that Jewish organizations need to both dramatically soften their boundaries and minimize the feeling of segmentation between "real life" and "Jewish life."[4]

You'll also notice that there are a number of large hearts inside the box. These represent the appreciation and excitement that the insiders feel for their community. They love it, and they believe that others would love it too if they would just give it a chance. This is, of course, a good thing. We all need community, and for clubs to remain strong, they need to continually recruit new members. The problem isn't the existence or popularity of the club; it is failing to also see the challenges inherent in the Club Model. A club works well for people who have a lot in common with one another, but what about Engagement Jews who have different Jewish stories than the Empowerment Jews who dominate the club? Or what about Jews with totally different forms of Jewish intelligences (as discussed in chapter 2), who have a hard time connecting with the programmatic offerings that work so well for those who are already connected?

The insider/outsider split also creates a problematic set of power dynamics that can make even simple things like recruitment difficult. Think about it. If you've ever been recruited by a group of people who are like you, it usually feels warm, inviting, and even personally validating. But if you've ever been recruited by a group of people who are different from you, it can feel totally different. Rather than feeling welcoming, recruitment from this kind of group can often come across as off-putting or coercive.[5]

For a great example of how complex and problematic the insider/outsider dynamic is, simply look at the way that newcomers are often greeted at Jewish events. The goal of having a greeter is to make new people feel more welcome, but something unintended can happen. When a new person arrives at some program, greeters often say things like "*We* are so happy *you* are here," "*We* want to welcome *you*," and "*We* have many great programs *you* will love." While explicitly the greeters are doing a wonderful job of welcoming a newcomer, implicitly they are repeatedly underscoring the distinction between "we" and "you." "We" are insiders. "You" are an outsider. "We" already feel comfortable. "You" need our help to feel comfortable. "We" have something to offer "you." "You" can help "us" by getting more involved or joining. Each time those words are used the impermeable boundary is accidentally reinforced.

There is another, more effective way to greet. Rather than using a greeting to make the event or organization the central focus of the conversation, a better approach is to make the person and the

"If you desire to be loved — then love others."

—The Baal Shem Tov

relationship the central focus instead.[6] This means that rather than talking about the Federation, the synagogue, or whatever organization you represent, start by getting to know the person. Good rules for these conversations are to avoid anything that sounds like a sales pitch and to leave out any of those well-meaning questions about Jewish involvement (like "Do you belong to a synagogue?" or "Have you been to other JCC family events?"). While you might just be trying to get to know them better, they can end up feeling interrogated, especially if they don't do the things you're asking about.

Instead, I suggest starting personally and informally. It could be something as simple as saying, "Hi, my name is Josh. What's yours? Tell me about yourself." Ideally the greeter not only welcomes the newcomer and begins the conversation, but also helps connect the newcomer to another person to continue the relationship-building process. The Orthodox Community at Penn Hillel (OCP) does this incredibly well. When there is someone who is new at services, they are greeted by several people. One of the community leaders then makes sure that the newcomer is seated with someone else. After this initial contact, there is always a next invitation: "Would you like to join us for a Shabbat meal?" After the Shabbat meal, the new person is then invited to be part of some initiative that is relationally driven. Many new people are then matched with a study partner (*chevruta*) for a program called Sarah and Abraham Memorial Sunday Night Learning (SNL). Every Sunday night, over one hundred students get together for free dinner and partnered study of everything from Talmud to the siddur and from Maimonides to Heschel. The students are masterful. They make people feel welcome, they establish relationships, and they match a person with a Jewish opportunity that feels right. All of this is done with genuine warmth and with no attempt to convert them to an Orthodox lifestyle.

Does better greeting solve all of the problems associated with the Club Model? Clearly not, but the real purpose of my sharing the Club Model with you is to make you aware of just how many complications come with it, especially if your organization is trying to engage new people. While our communities still need clubs and even membership organizations with boundaries, the key takeaway here is that we should not assume that the Club Model can meet the needs of many different types of Jews. If we are really serious about engagement and about building smarter organizations, then we will need a model that will allow for a more complex notion of how community works.

Model # 2: The Outreach Model

The Outreach Model represents the next step in the evolution of Jewish engagement. Examine figure 2 and see what you notice about the way this community functions:

1. What's the same and what's different from the Club Model?
2. What does the placement of the various lines and arrows tell us about how people relate to one another and where Jewish life takes place?

The Outreach Model is similar to the Club Model in a number of ways. They are both focused on branded Jewish institutions surrounded by an impermeable boundary. If you look at the ways the arrows are arranged, you can see that the goal in this model is still to recruit people to leave

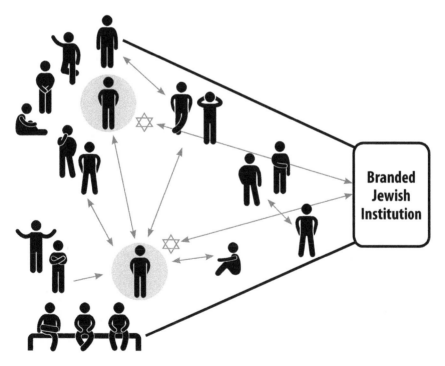

Figure 2. The Outreach Model

where they are in order to join the community or the activities taking place within the confines of a Jewish institution.

"There remained two men in the camp: the name of the one was Eldad, and the name of the other Medad; and the spirit rested on them... and they prophesied in the camp. Some were bother by their leadership, but Moses responded, "Would that all the Lord's people were prophets, that the Lord would put God's spirit on them!'"

—Adapted from Numbers 11:26–29

The only difference here is that the Outreach Model has a more sophisticated strategy for recruitment. Rather than just trying to attract new people, in the Outreach Model the organization sends a couple of insiders out of the box to build relationships with the people who are not already "involved." Notice the two people with gray circles around them and Jewish stars near them—they represent the recruiters.

There are some improvements here on the Club Model. By sending "cool" and diverse recruiters out, there is a better chance of reaching new people. This model is also more relationship driven. As you look at the different arrows, you will notice that some of the smaller arrows are actually connecting people to each other and not just to the institution. This is a positive thing. It means that new social networks and communities are starting to form outside of a formal Jewish space.

That said, this model is less than ideal, because the goal is still to recruit others to join the branded Jewish institution. As you get closer to the institution, the lines narrow and there is less and less room for diversity. This highlights the fact that a strong focus on recruitment inevitably means less of a focus on helping every Jew find new ways to connect to Jewish life. Another shortcoming of this model is that while Judaism now exists outside the building, it isn't yet independent—it still relies on the official outreach people to make it happen. In a more fully mature model of Jewish engagement, the organization could actually unlock the power of the different social networks so that more people could become creators of Jewish life.[7] The more creators, the more vibrant and more accessible Jewish life becomes.

Model #3: The Open Book Model

The third model represents the next stage in the development of an engagement organization and is called the Open Book Model. Look at figure 3 and notice the way this new community functions:

1. What's the same and what's different between this model and the first two? How has the role of a "branded Jewish organization" changed?
2. What does the fact that there are no arrows in this model mean about the way an organization understands the goals of engagement?

At first glance you can see that there is no branded institution and there are no arrows. This represents a radical departure from what we have seen in the other models of community. The Open Book Model seems to have shed all of the institutional motivations. Rather than focusing on recruitment, affiliation, or attendance, the goal of the Open Book Model is to meet people where they are and to bring Judaism to them. Instead of clubs,

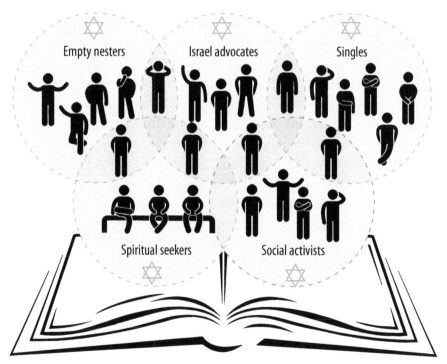

Figure 3. The Open Book Model, showing a way to map different social networks by interest and stage of life.

this model, depicts networks that have more fluid boundaries and are interconnected. Rather than providing a one-size-fits-all approach, in this model the role of the Jewish organization is to empower different networks of Jews to create Jewish experiences for themselves. And because different styles of Judaism exist in each network, this kind of empowerment leads to an increase in the diversity of Jewish opportunities.

This shift in orientation also implies that the organization is no longer only a service provider, but also a promoter of Jewish empowerment and Jewish experience in smaller, non-institutionally based communities. Perhaps most importantly, this model actually sustains more Judaism, as it exists vibrantly in many different circles. Now the way an organization creates community isn't by funneling a large number of Jews to one space or program, but by bringing Jewish life to all sorts of networks and then finding ways to weave the different networks together to make sure that they remain overlapped.[8]

You also may have noticed that I changed my language once we started talking about the Open Book Model. Rather than using the word "community," I am now using the word "network." That shift is intentional and informed by the distinctions made by social scientists between the two words. Communities by nature tend to be more fixed, with more noticeable boundaries and shared cultural norms, while networks tend to be more porous and transient. Networks can change and shift as needed. Communities are formed organically, but networks can be constructed intentionally to achieve a purpose. The function of a leader is also different for communities and networks. In a community, leaders have some kind of formal distinction or title. They may also have a particular talent, specialized training, or financial capital that assists them in their leadership role. Networks, on the other hand, are shaped and directed by people with extraordinary social capital—people who are connectors or influencers. Communities have many positive characteristics. They can create a sense of safety and security, they encourage the sharing of resources, and they can promote collaboration toward a shared objective.[9] But communities also place a large emphasis on "we," in a way that requires members to give up a degree of individual autonomy for the health and well-being of the collective. Networks, by contrast, make more room for the "me," because they are more about how people connect with each other without traditional boundaries and can continue to function even with a much higher degree of individuality among the members.

Just by this brief description, you can see how networks could play a huge role in helping organizations reach more Engagement Jews who are post-institutional in their orientation. The porous and transient nature of networks, which could be seen as a weakness for an institution, is attractive to a person looking to explore Judaism without making a full commitment to a community. Networks by nature are easier to join because you only need a relationship and a shared interest to get connected. Usually there are fewer boundaries and lower requirements for initiation.

Another aspect of the Open Book Model is that there is a shift from large groups to small groups. This is important because large groups tend to be more sparsely connected, while small groups tend to be densely connected.[10] Imagine a huge Federation gala event or a large synagogue service. The gathering can often feel large and impersonal. So what do people in these situations do to feel more comfortable? They find a small group of people they already know to connect with so the event feels more intimate. This works really well if you're a regular in Jewish communal activities, because you know enough people to find your own circle. But what if you're not a regular and you don't have those social connections? Then large groups just feel unwelcoming. That's why when it comes to engagement work, small groups are an essential tool for reaching new people. It is much easier to welcome and connect a new person to a small group than to a large one. But that is only the first step in deploying the Open Book Model. The larger goal is to build many small groups that are dense and intimate and then link them to other groups (through relationships) so that you end up with a network of networks.[11]

The Open Book Model also creates a new method for marketing. In the Club Model, the way an organization markets is to broadcast information as far and wide as possible. This could be via mailings, fliers, or newspaper or Facebook ads. Whatever the format, the method is the same—a small group of leaders tries to communicate with the largest possible number of individuals to encourage participation. Because the Open Book Model functions through networks, the communication strategy works differently. The networks themselves serve as amplifiers and filters for information.[12] This means that the way we find out about events is not through mass publicity but from talking to friends and acquaintances in our social network.

In large part, this is what really happens anyway when Jewish institutions do mass publicity. While you may get an invitation in the mail, the real decision of whether to go to an event is usually based on conversations and connections you have with your friends. One of the radical aspects of the Open Book Model is that it might actually make traditional forms of publicity obsolete. When JRP is really working well, no advertising is necessary. If Rebecca Kaplan is hosting a Shabbat dinner at her house, it is not a program targeted for the general public. It's a dinner party for her friends. Everyone who needs to know about it will already know simply by being part of her network. This also highlights the fact that in the Open Book Model there is no assumption that the goal of an organization is to get each network to do the same things at the same time. Each network can operate independently. While it may seem like chaos at first, in reality this level of independence actually helps generate a dramatic increase in the amount of Jewish life taking place in any given area.

Now that we understand a little more about how networks function, how are they formed? Some of them already exist—think of the naturally occurring networks of like-minded people who are already friends or who all live in the same neighborhood. For these kinds of preexisting networks, the role of the organization is to map them out and then try to find ways to empower them to be creators of Jewish life for themselves. Some networks do not exist yet. In this case, the role of the organization is to help these people find each other. For example, imagine that a great Federation professional knows a large number of different Jews who are all interested in the same kind of philanthropy, but they don't know each other. In this case, the professional can serve as the bridge builder who links all of these people together, forming a network that didn't previously exist.

On campus, Hillel does both of these things all the time. Often we encounter a group of friends who all run in the same social circles. They may live together, study together, and socialize together, but they are not yet engaged in Jewish life together. In this case, Hillel's job is to help encourage them to take that step to explore their Judaism together. But for students who are both not engaged in Jewish life and do not have a Jewish social network, Hillel staff may take a different approach. In this case, we work hard first to build relationships with these students and then to help connect them with others who are in a similar situation. For example, if a Hillel staff member were to meet many students who all feel disengaged and guilty about not enjoying services when they went on Shabbat, rather than trying to create a program to solve that problem she could instead connect these students with each other and help them to create a venue to explore these feelings or to gain new tools that would actually help them get more out of services. In this case, Hillel's job is to leverage their vast array of student relationships in order to help like-minded people find each other and create new networks.

Another question to consider is how we, as organizational leaders, understand the different kinds of interests and characteristics that act as glue for the different circles. For example, in figure 3, the circles are determined by mapping different interests: there are the pro-Israel Jews, the baseball-loving Jews, the guitar-playing Jews, and so on. Mapping by interest is the most basic way to use this model. You could also map out different networks based on the stage of life people are in—young professionals, families with children, empty nesters. The advantage of mapping networks based on stage of life is that it can help your organization be responsive to the different schedules, needs, and interests that people have in different moments of their lives.

"God of the spirits [of all flesh]—Why is this expression used? Moses said to God: 'Lord of the Universe! The personality of each person is revealed to you, and no two are alike. Appoint over them a leader who will accommodate each person according to his individual character.'"

—Rashi on Numbers 27:16

An even deeper way to apply this model is to map different types of Jews by using the theory of multiple Jewish intelligences discussed in chapter 2. Rather than mapping them by age or interest, you can map them based on how they process and understand the meaning and purpose of Jewishness (see chapter 2 for a fuller discussion of how this could be applied).

There is some legitimate concern that if we continue this methodology to its logical end, we might encourage people to associate only with people who are just like them, leading them away from any sense of collective purpose or identity. While it's true that the Open Book Model does allow for more customization and a stronger focus on micro-communities, in its most sophisticated form, organizations would also work to ensure that these networks are porous and overlapping so that different groups don't end up being isolated from one another.

Bonding and Bridging Capital

Depending on what kind of experience you've had in Jewish communal life, you might be wondering, "Is this really a new idea? Isn't the Open Book Model just like what synagogues and Federations are already doing with *chavurot* and affinity groups?" And the answer is that it depends. The idea of Jewish organizations bringing together smaller micro-communities as a way of helping people connect in a more intimate and personal way is not new. This is a model that was pioneered by megachurches and is used by many Jewish organizations today.[13] It functions by increasing the depth of connection and trust within a relatively homogeneous group. Social scientists call this "bonding capital."[14] These types of *chavurot* or affinity groups tend to be most successful for Jews who are already connected to Jewish life (such as Empowerment Jews who are already members of synagogue and/or leaders in Federation).

What is different about the Open Book Model is that it is also used for reaching Engagement Jews and therefore must go beyond the use of bonding capital. For the Open Book Model to be most effective, the organization should also find ways to connect people from heterogeneous Jewish backgrounds who are part of different social circles—this is called "bridging capital."[15] For example, a Federation could bring together twenty preexisting donors who don't yet know each other to become a network that learns together, participates in different Federation activities together, and eventually becomes a group of friends. After that group is connected and inspired, the Federation would then encourage each of the members of the network to reach out and engage others they know who are not yet connected (this is when bridging capital is deployed). The next step is key: rather than meeting new people in order to get them to join the original group (i.e., to grow it from twenty

to two hundred people), in this methodology each of the twenty original leaders would now also become a convener of his or her own new
network. So rather than building a larger club of two hundred people,
the organization might end up with twenty smaller groups of ten people
each. While the Federation is still the foundation that helps the system
work, each new leader is not just part of a network but also the creator
of another network. As you can imagine, these processes can dramatically expand the number and diversity of opportunities to connect with
Jewish life.

The second major difference that separates the Open Book Model
from *chavurot* and affinity groups is the Open Book Model's emphasis
on empowerment. In many instances, synagogues and Federations build
these groups and then continue to act as the service provider for them. A
great example of this is the way Federations tend to run programs like the
Men's Cabinet or the Renaissance Group. These affinity groups do a great
job of building community, training leaders, and growing donors, but the
professionals are usually responsible for planning and running the events.
In the Open Book Model, the role of the professional is to build the group
and then help them to become a fully empowered, self-sustaining network
that can generate Jewish life for themselves and for others.

In this way, both *chavurot* and affinity groups and the Open Book
Model play important roles in creating micro-communities that make
Jewish organizations feel more intimate and accessible, but they do so in
different ways.

Which Is the Best Model for Your Community?

Which of these three models is best for your community? The short answer
is, it depends. There are many organizations that will consciously choose
to remain a Club Model, and as I have said, that is a good thing, because
communities need clubs. But for organizations that want to do engagement work and to reach larger numbers of Jews with more diverse Jewish
backgrounds, the Open Book Model is preferable.

My real goal in using these models is not to come up with simple
answers to solve the Jewish community's complicated problems; rather,
it's to continually expand the possibilities for how people can connect

to Jewish life. Ideally, we can use the Open Book Model in a way that is expansive and flexible enough to incorporate the other two models when they are needed. In other words, in its purest form, the Open Book Model allows for some of those circles to be porous networks and for some of them to be traditional communities that look more like the Club Model or the Outreach Model.

Questions for Further Consideration

1. How can these models be used to spark discussions among different leadership groups in your organization?

2. How do the different models validate and/or challenge some of the assumptions your organization has about how community works?

3. Which of these models most resembles the work your organization currently does?

4. In looking at the Open Book Model, how would you map out the different networks reachable by your organizations (both the preexisting ones and the networks that you would like to convene)?

5. Which way of determining these networks works best for you? By interest? By stage of life? By different types of Jewish intelligence?

6. When you map out the different networks, which new groups come into focus that your organization may want to better engage?

7. What would it take in terms of staff, money, and relationships for your organization to actually engage these new groups?

6

Building an Impact Organization

If you want to see what an organization really cares about, take a look at what they measure.

> A local Jewish newspaper in a major Midwestern city published a special issue with a *U.S. News*–style ranking of the different synagogues in town. The ranking system was not complicated. The paper created a long list of possible services or functions that a synagogue could have, and gave one point for each of the criteria that was met. The list included features like having a gift shop, cleanliness of the building, quality of the outdoor play space, and number of children in the religious school. It gave points for the existence of adult learning programs but did nothing to measure how many people participated or how much they learned. Ironically, or sadly, the paper did not give points for anything related to prayer or religious life. But it did count the numbers of members who "belonged" to a given synagogue.

In the end, what did the newspaper actually measure? It treated the synagogues almost like country clubs, ranking them based on their facilities and services offered. All of these measures are more about institutional health and budget size than about the organization's capacity to make a difference in people's lives.[1] Gift shops are nice, but they don't inspire people to live more meaningful and successful lives.

So what's the right thing to measure and the best way to define success? There is really just one thing that should count—

Impact. Impact. Impact.

The real purpose for every synagogue, JCC, Federation, and Hillel is to make a positive impact on people's lives and the lives of the communities they engage. The particular type of impact can take on almost any form. It can be about prayer, community service, philanthropy, or Jewish survival. The key is that the organization has to be focused on making a positive difference in people's lives, not on keeping the organization alive.[2]

This may seem obvious, yet so many organizations struggle to stay focused on what really matters, because real life takes over and the work that is urgent (like operations, budgets, annual campaigns, and programmatic calendars) takes precedence over what is important.[3] Day-to-day and week-to-week, these are the issues that require the most attention, because they are the lifeblood of what organizations do and how they sustain their existence. This is especially true for organizations that feel like they are in decline.

While there may have been a time when the organized Jewish community was so secure that it could get away with being overly focused on institutional health, that is no longer the case today.[4] American Judaism and the way that Jews relate to institutions is changing fast, and people want meaning and personal impact. This means that for organizations to continue to be relevant, they need to find ways to start to track and measure the right things so that they can become the organizations they want to be.

Invert the Values Pyramid

The first step in changing what your organization measures is to invert the values pyramid. Rather than placing the needs of the institution—things like membership, donations, and attendance—at the top of the values pyramid, place the needs of the individual or communities you engage at the top—things like meaning, inspiration, and a sense of belonging (figure 4).

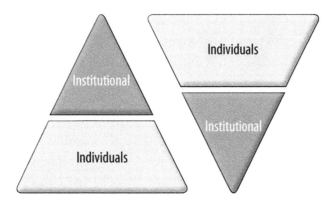

Figure 4. Inverting the values pyramid

When organizations are focused more on the needs of the institution than on the needs of the individuals or communities they represent, they are destined to struggle in today's world. A real-life example of how this plays out comes from a young couple who lived in Los Angeles. This couple was looking to become more active in Jewish life, to find deeper meaning and purpose in their lives. But when they began to explore local synagogues, their experience was stressful and off-putting:

> As soon as people found out that we were "unaffiliated," the sales pitch for joining the temple started in full force. The whole thing felt wrong. The pitch wasn't really about what we wanted or needed. People would say things like "We are always looking for young families to join," or "We have a special discount on membership dues right now for young families." We felt like they were selling us on a gym membership rather than inviting us to be part of an intentional community.

In the case of this young couple, the organizations missed their opportunities to connect because they were more focused on securing a new set of membership dues than on fostering a new relationship. This happens all the time in other Jewish organizations as well, and I believe it is a direct outgrowth of a values pyramid that is out of alignment with the organization's core mission. It is a vicious cycle that leads to missed opportunities time and again. The more an organization is focused on membership, attendance, and donations, the more it ends up treating people like a means to an end, which turns people off. This, of course, leads to lower membership, attendance, and donations, which reinforces the organization's misplaced focus, starting the cycle over again.

"Much has been spoken and written in our midst about nation and society, about the community and its institutions. But the individual has been lost sight of."

—Abraham Joshua Heschel

This dynamic can also be seen in the natural evolution that occurs with the annual events that fill an organization's calendar. Usually programs begin with some real need and purpose in mind. However, as the years pass, programs tend to become institutionalized; they fill some empty dates on the calendar, or they continue annually out of habit.[5] One of the worst stories I have heard about a program that had outlived its time and purpose was sponsored by a large Federation on the East Coast:

> There was an annual event that tried to recruit a huge number of Jews to engage in community service on a particular Sunday in the spring. Each year there was tremendous pressure to get people to participate, and each year enthusiasm dwindled. Someone at the top of the organizational pyramid was excited about the idea of Mitzvah Day and pushed the rest of the Federation staff to make this event a success. This pressure then trickled down to the various agencies funded by the Federation. The leadership of these agencies, in turn, put pressure on their staff, who, in the case of Hillel, put pressure on the students. When the big Sunday arrived, no one seemed truly excited. Nonetheless, students, Hillel board members, and community donors showed up at the home of an elderly and impoverished Jewish woman early that morning. Her first response to the arrival of the volunteers was "Why are you here? I told the Federation I didn't want to participate."
>
> The story actually gets worse from here. The volunteers began a project of painting her kitchen, only to find out that they did not have enough time or supplies to finish. When

the bus arrived to collect them, all of the volunteers left, even though her kitchen was only half painted. In the end, they left the woman's home worse off than they found it, and she stood at the front door cursing the volunteers as they boarded the buses to go home.

This is a tragic story. The organization was so intent on executing a program and getting people to show up that they totally lost sight of the original purpose, which was to actually help Jews in need. In the end, everyone involved lost. The Federation came out of this program looking terrible, and both the volunteers and the people they were trying to help were turned off and angry. While this story stands out as a particularly egregious example of what happens when organizations focus on the wrong thing, less dramatic examples of this take place every day in Jewish communities all over the country.

> "Good deeds done for self-interest and not for their own sake are better off not being done at all."
> —The Baal Shem Tov

To get our organizations to invert the values pyramid and place the needs and interests of individuals above the needs of the institution, we as leaders have to be disciplined and change the questions we ask. Rather than focusing on increasing participation among teens or young families or on finding new ways to increase attendance or donations, we could focus first on how we could make a significant difference in people's lives. This starts by asking ourselves how to better understand the spiritual, moral, and personal needs of the different age groups that we seek to engage, including youth and young families:[6]

- How can Jewish values, rituals, and communities help people live richer, more contented, and ethical lives?
- What kind of resources (both time and money) does the organization need to successfully build personal relationships with these various populations?
- How can philanthropy help Jews make a difference in the world, find personal meaning, and live more interconnected lives with those in their community?

This shift in language is more than simply semantics. The way we speak, the way we think, and what we do are all linked.[7] Change the way someone speaks and you can change the world. Just think how different the experience would have been for the young couple mentioned above if the synagogue leaders approaching them had focused on them rather than on the needs of the synagogue? Would that annual Mitzvah Day have happened in the same way if the organization had focused on the experience of the volunteers and the person in need rather than on simply making this year's event bigger than last year's?

By simply articulating a different set of goals and inverting the values pyramid, the conversation becomes more visionary and forward thinking. Much of the fear and trepidation organizations feel seems to evaporate as a result. Board meetings become more exciting and less contentious when the focus is on the mission and not the institution's needs. While this shift in focus may seem unrealistic or overly idealistic at first glance, the bottom line is that when you get it right in terms of making an impact, you will be able to attract the money and talent necessary to sustain real transformation. Of course you cannot ignore the business aspects of running an organization. But can you really solve the problems of money, membership, facility, and staff without fixing the deeper issues?

Inverting the Values Pyramid at IKAR

Rabbi Sharon Brous

Years ago I read a piece by David Steindl-Rast, a Benedictine monk, that perfectly articulated the challenge and opportunities of faith communities today. Religion, he writes, is like an erupting volcano: the lava flowing down the sides of the mountain is fiery, powerful, dangerous, "gushing forth red hot from the depths of mystical consciousness." But the stream of lava quickly cools off. A couple hundred years pass, and what was once alive is now dead rock, devoid of all traces of life. "Doctrine becomes doctrinaire. Morals become moralistic. Ritual becomes ritualistic.... All are layers of ash deposits and volcanic rock that separate us from the fiery magma deep down below" (see "The Mystical Core of Organized Religion" and *Lunch with Bokara*).

Religious systems and institutions begin as containers designed to hold the sacred experience, preserve its power, and extend its reverberations. But these containers, because one can touch and mold and compulsively ruminate over them, quickly start to obscure the very core they were designed to preserve. When that happens, rather than giving people access to profound spiritual and religious inspiration, the containers themselves become an obstacle to inspiration.

This is precisely what's happening in American religious life today, thus the unprecedented disaffection, defection, and overriding sense of disinterest among American Jews, especially young ones. The silver lining is that it's not Judaism they are rejecting. They don't reject Jewish identity, community, or rituals. They don't reject Jewish ideas or even God. They reject a twentieth-century iteration of Jewish religious life that feels too many layers away from the sacred fire. It feels devoid of life, passion, spiritual challenge. American Jewish institutions have focused too much on the container (formalities, rules, boundaries, and comfortable scripts) and not enough on the fire—the soul and spirit, the mystical core.

To free ourselves of the dead rock and ash deposit of twentieth-century institutional religious life, we have to engage counter-instinctually. We have to reclaim discomfort as essential to growth. Take prayer, for example. Our services have become so rehearsed and perfunctory that they rarely pierce the surface, let alone penetrate the heart. In Heschel's words, we read the prayer book as if reading paragraphs in *Roget's Thesaurus*. "Of course," he writes, "they are offered plenty of responsive reading, but there is little responsiveness to what they read. No one knows how to shed a tear. No one is ready to invest a sigh. Is there no tear in their souls?" (see *Moral Grandeur and Spiritual Audacity*). How do we create, once again, the space for tears in our services? For movement, for spontaneity and vulnerability?

One of the central challenges of religious life today is to reclaim and then reanimate the prayer experience. One Friday afternoon a few years after we started IKAR, I realized that we had hit our stride in services, and our spiritual revolution had become routinized. Our *Kabbalat Shabbat* was losing its dynamism, its sense of surprise. People were still coming, yes, but my goal wasn't to fill seats but to move hearts.

So about an hour before services, we decided to experiment. We moved into a room about a third the size, removed all the chairs, and posted signs that read: Discomfort Is Better Than Boredom. A few hundred people arrived for Shabbat services that evening. They were confused, agitated, and annoyed. Many refused even to step into the room. It was a dismal failure … so we tried again a couple of weeks later. The second time, everyone came into the room, but they stood in straight rows, stiff as soldiers. By the third try, people moved. They danced and sang. Some cried. It was a breakthrough moment for our community. Many told me they had never davened until that service—it was the first time they felt free enough to express what was in their hearts.

We have become so habituated to our limitations—environment, formal rules of a prayer service ("please rise / please be seated")—that our spiritual muscles have atrophied. It takes a lot of will to awaken the soul, but we can reclaim our spiritual freedom.

Discomfort wakes us up. It takes the community—and the leadership—by surprise. If we are willing to fail publicly, to experiment when there is no reasonable assurance that we'll succeed, we can build spiritually vital communities. Sometimes the best moments of our services come when we start on the wrong page or in the wrong key, laugh, and adjust or stop in middle of a service that's not working and ask that everyone stand up and move around, come join us in the middle of the room, or talk about what's not working and start over. We try every Shabbat to take some risk, dive into discomfort, and honor the learning that comes from failure. This is the way that we begin to clear away some of the ash and drill through rock to find the sacred heart once again.

Getting Beyond Program

Let's say that we've all accepted the premise that we want to invert the values pyramid. How do we accomplish that in practical terms?

We all love programs, and all organizations will need to continue to create them. When they are done right, programs are transformative and highly impactful. But in all honesty, many programs exist simply because they have been happening every year up until now. Often leadership is so busy and overworked that they have no time to think of something new to do. Rather than doing *nothing*, the same annual program takes place, even if it may not really be accomplishing its original goal.

One of the ways to counteract much of what's wrong with the classic Program Model is to adopt a Community Development Model instead. In the Community Development Model, both the purpose of the event and how it's developed are turned on their heads. Rather than measuring success by the number of people who show up, the Community Development Model is focused on the impact of an event. This can be measured by the level of Jewish inspiration, by the amount of Jewish learning or Jewish growth that takes place, and by the number of new relationships created. Traditional programs are often "one-off" events, while community development

> "The end of a tradition does not necessarily mean that traditional concepts have lost their power over the minds of men. On the contrary, it seems that this power of well-worn notions and categories becomes more tyrannical as the tradition loses its living force and as the memory of the beginning recedes; it may even reveal its full coercive force only after its end has come and men no longer even rebel against it."
>
> —Hannah Arendt

events are part of a larger initiative that has a built-in mechanism for connecting people to their next Jewish experience.[8]

The first planning question in the Program Model is "What should we do?" while in the Community Development Model the first question is "Who should we talk to?" Rather than leaders brainstorming about what kind of program would be great, leadership now begins by brainstorming who they should reach out to speak with. Now, the process of envisioning the event doesn't happen at a committee meeting with a select group of leaders; it happens in many one-on-one conversations. The number of people who have a stake in the event's success grows exponentially. In the Program Model, leaders plan events for participants. In the Community Development Model, the gap between leaders and participants begins to evaporate. Events are planned in partnership with the community, created by a large social network. The institution is still there, but rather than leading from out front and providing the experience, the institution is facilitating from behind, empowering people to create their own Jewish experiences.

Program Model	Community Development Model
Goal is attendance	Goal is impact
Often "one-off" event	Part of a larger initiative
Motivation is institutional	Motivation is personal
First planning question is "What should we do?"	First planning question is "Who should we talk to?"
Creates a gap between formal leaders and passive participants	Planned in partnership with others

The Power and Peril of Tracking, Data, and Metrics

The next step in building an impact organization is creating a new system for tracking the kind of information you need and then crunching that data necessary to measure your success. But how do you measure success? Both in life and in building Jewish organizations, the answer to this question is often elusive and confounding. The conversation about how to measure the impact of different Jewish organizations and their programmatic offerings seems to be never-ending, and there are, of course, several conflicting approaches to consider.

One approach resists the idea of metrics altogether. For this group, metrics are soul-crushing numbers that negate the transcendent work of building Jewish life. Some claim that the work we do is fundamentally immeasurable. I have heard many people in this camp cite the famous quip from Supreme Court Justice Potter Stuart that while I may not be able to tell you what it is, "I know it when I see it."[9] Good Jewish leaders know how to do their work, and they know success when they see it.

The other approach is the belief that data holds an almost mystical power to diagnose and solve all of the challenges facing the Jewish nonprofit sector. For this group, the right tracking, data, and metrics can prove which type of Jewish interventions help inspire long-term Jewish affiliation, in-marriage, or support for the State of Israel. They can tell organizations how to attract new members or raise more money on an annual basis and can help donors distinguish between which initiatives to fund and which not to fund.

The truth about metrics and data is of course somewhere in between these two approaches. When tracking and data are used in the right way, it can be transformative for an organization. But if used in the wrong way, it can certainly damage your organization. It is not uncommon that small Jewish nonprofits are required to track data based on the needs and interests of outside funders or partner organizations in a way that is incredibly labor intensive and often fails to capture the information most relevant for the organization itself.[10]

At Penn Hillel, we have actually started to use data collection and metrics in a way that is tremendously helpful. We have figured out some very simple ways to gather the information we need that helps us measure the right things. Today, we can track how many people we are reaching, sort that number by different types of initiatives (prayer versus Israel; community service versus Jewish education), and run reports that tell us how frequently different people are reached over time. This means that we have concrete evidence of how many students we reach each year and how often we engage them. Knowing what's really going on actually makes our work simpler, more focused, and more achievable. Rather than trying to be all things to all people all the time, data actually helps concretize the work.[11] For example, if we can see that sixty-three freshmen were highly connected to Jewish life in September and October and then dropped off, we can stop thinking in terms of just reaching more freshmen and instead focus on the places where we can make the biggest difference. So while it may be intimidating to reach everyone, the goal of reaching out personally to those sixty-three students and trying to reengage them feels highly achievable.

By measuring student engagement, we can even start to get a clearer picture of whether different staff are spending their time on the right things and if they are being successful. After a few years of gathering good data, we now have benchmarks of what our staff members should be able to accomplish in a given year. This makes it easier to communicate with our staff about the work and helps us set real and measurable expectations for performance. In addition, the data helps us communicate with our funders and stakeholders. Rather than simply telling people that we had a "great semester," Penn Hillel can use specifics; for example, we might be able to report that by October 31, our staff had reached 73 percent of Jewish freshmen and that the new engagement professional we hired for an experimental position has reached three times as many freshmen as our existing staff. This data also allows us to demonstrate that each time our staff has a meaningful contact with a student—like a coffee-date with Jewish conversation—the student gets more engaged in in Jewish life on campus. These are real, empirical measurements of Penn Hillel's success. Later on in this chapter, I will go into more depth about how Penn Hillel measures its impact.

Three Simple Ways to Measure Impact

Once an organization has inverted its value pyramid and shifted from a Program Model to a Community Development Model, the next step is to begin to track and measure the impact that the organization can effect.

How to measure impact is, of course, the million-dollar question that many social scientists and Jewish organizational leaders are grappling with. There are many experts trained in social science who specialize in helping evaluate the impact of different Jewish initiatives. The problem is that they are expensive, and most synagogues, JCCs, Federations, and Hillels cannot afford to spend $25,000 to $50,000 to hire an expert outside evaluator to measure the impact of their work.

For those of us who cannot afford to hire outside evaluators, I want to share with you a few tools that work for us and that you can use for your organization regardless of budget. Also, full disclosure, as a practitioner who is not a social scientist, I have a different set of goals in mind when it comes time to measure and track. I don't need objective, scientific proof; I need some basic data and tools that are good enough to accomplish two important goals:

1. **Measurement for management:** These kinds of tools give the professionals what they need to know to better understand, evaluate, and improve their organization's ability to fulfill its mission.
2. **Measurement for evaluation:** These kinds of tools help your organization prove the impact of its work to the larger community of investors, stakeholders, and partners.

Following are three models that we use at Penn Hillel.

Model #1: Defining a Meaningful Jewish Experience

Once we move beyond measuring program attendance and membership, what do we want to measure next? For Hillel, the goal is creating "meaningful Jewish experiences," a phrase that has no clear-cut definition. In order to come up with some parameters for what constitutes a meaningful Jewish experience, Hillel International began a series of conversations with Jewish professionals, with board members, and then with students. After hundreds of conversations and listening forums, something started to emerge. There were four common characteristics that seemed to be present across the board when people told their stories (figure 5).[12] Most meaningful Jewish experiences seemed to result in each of the following:

1. **Positive Jewish memory:** Whether from family seders, services in the woods at summer camp, or the first visit to the Negev in Israel, the most impactful Jewish experiences create a warm and powerful memory.[13] Positive Jewish memory is crucial in engagement work in order to overcome all of the negative Jewish memories people have about Hebrew school, long synagogue services, or cliquey Hillel Shabbat dinners.
2. **Increased Jewish knowledge:** This includes more foundational knowledge, like basic literacy and skill acquisition, as well as more

theoretical forms of knowledge, like conceptual frameworks for understanding the nuance of Jewish ideas, values, and history.

3. **Increased Jewish self-confidence:** A sense of Jewish insecurity is one of the most potent impediments to successful Jewish engagement. It is very hard for people who are confident, successful, and self-actualized in other areas of their lives to walk into a Jewish space and feel ignorant and out of place. Therefore, increasing the levels of Jewish self-confidence is essential to a successful engagement strategy.

4. **Increased connectedness to other Jews:** One of Hillel's operating principles is that "nothing meaningful happens outside of community." Whether it's Torah study, community service, or spiritual practice, a feeling of connectedness to other Jews is necessary for any high-impact experience and for building a sustainable form of Judaism outside of institutions.[14]

"Nothing meaningful happens outside of community."

When a Jewish experience comprises all or most of these four components, it has the power to advance an individual's or community's level of Jewish ownership. As people's ownership of Jewish experience increases,

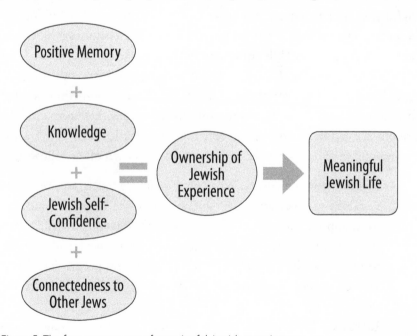

Figure 5. The four components of meaningful Jewish experiences

it is more likely that they will live a meaningful and vibrant Jewish life, which is our ultimate goal.

Imagine what our Jewish communities would look like if we applied these four criteria to every programmatic initiative, life-cycle event, and leadership experience? If Jewish organizations could find ways to seriously and intentionally apply these criteria to *b'nei mitzvah* training, board membership, youth group events, and prayer experiences, how much richer would each of them be? Certainly it would make each of these experiences higher impact.

Model #2: The Theory of ABC Goals

Another model that can be helpful in both setting goals for an initiative and then measuring the impact of that initiative is commonly referred to as ABC goals (attitude, behavior, cognition). When an experience positively affects these three categories, real progress occurs:

1. **Attitude:** The degree to which an experience can change how people feel and think about their Judaism and how it affects their level of Jewish self-confidence, Jewish appreciation, and connectedness to other Jews.
2. **Behavior:** This is a measurement of how an experience leads to a change in someone's subsequent behavior—for example, the degree to which a business ethics class affects the choices a person makes at the office or the way that a community service project inspires someone to become more active with social justice issues.
3. **Cognition:** This measures growth in Jewish literacy, knowledge, conceptual understanding, and skills that people can use in constructing their own Jewish lives and in being part of a community.

When put into action, the ABC Model can serve as a prompt to help organizational leaders deepen the success of any programmatic initiative by adding new impact goals that are likely to promote Jewish growth. Let's take, for example, the kind of young leadership groups run by many Federations across North America. Traditionally, the goal of this initiative is to create a pipeline of future volunteer leaders and donors. But when we apply the ABC Model to this initiative, we can accomplish much more.

When it comes to attitudes, in addition to inspiring people to more deeply appreciate the work of the Federation, the initiative would also aim to foster general inspiration about Judaism. Rather than focusing just on ways to navigate the various Jewish agencies that comprise a community, there could also be a focus on tools that would help empower participants to live richer and deeper Jewish lives. This may include increased confidence in hosting a Shabbat meal, a better understanding of the library of great Jewish books, or greater comfort with the Hebrew language. In terms of behavior, in addition to hoping that participants will donate to the Federation and join its leadership structure, this initiative could also inspire people to become creators of Jewish life for others, to read more Jewish books, and to apply the practical wisdom they have learned from these texts to their lives both at home and at work. This model could also be applied to a youth group, an adult education class, or a prayer experience.

Model #3: Measuring Breadth and Depth

We use the first two models at Penn Hillel today, and they frame the entire way we do our work—shaping our mission and guiding both our short-term and long-term programmatic and staffing strategies. They help us to discern which types of initiatives are worth investing in and which ones to pass on. We use these two models to help us train staff and student leaders and to provoke big-picture thinking about our mission and goals each year.

But we also employ a third model that ties the first two together. In order to make this last model come to life, I want to share with you the way we used it at Penn Hillel for a JRP program called the Campus Entrepreneurs Initiative (CEI).[15] In addition to using the ways of measuring we have already talked about, Penn Hillel also sets goals that measure both the depth and the breadth of this initiative every year. It's important to know that the goals are developed and expressed so that staff, student interns, and funders all know the expectations from the beginning.

The depth goals measure the impact the initiative has on students. We gather this information by asking student interns to fill out a survey at the end of each semester. These questions mirror some of the goals discussed in the two models above. We use a fee service called Google Forms, and we ask a series of questions that looks something like this:

- To what degree did this initiative help you gain more Jewish self-confidence?
- To what degree did you feel a sense of community of CEI interns?
- Please rate your overall excitement about the initiative.
- Please rate the degree to which the Jewish learning helped you gain new Jewish knowledge.

Students are asked to rank themselves on a Likert scale from 1 to 5, with 1 being low and 5 being high. When we crunch the data, we can evaluate how well the initiative is doing in terms of meeting its goals. If students report answers that average between 4 and 5 on the scale, we know we're doing something right. If we see that the numbers are lower, we know something is off.

We also set breadth goals each year that measure how many students will be touched by the CEI program in addition to the student interns themselves. Those goals look something like this:

- JRP staff recruit seventeen sophomores in the Greek system who have a high degree of social capital in their respective fraternities or sororities.
- Each student intern will build relationships with sixty students who have not been previously engaged by Hillel.
- Each student intern will create a programmatic initiative that will generate three events per semester.
- The total reach of the CEI Program will be at least 1,020 students.
- All student interns should be Engagement Jews who are not already engaged by Hillel or JRP (20 percent with little to no past Jewish engagement, 60 percent with little or no Jewish engagement since bar or bat mitzvah age, 20 percent with more post-involvement but not yet on campus).

At first, the whole idea of collecting and using data was totally overwhelming. But once we established our own system, we found that even with relatively limited resources, Penn Hillel can really measure its impact on students. Each semester, we review this data to chart our progress and refine our model. Supervisors look through the data with the people they supervise as part of their semi-annual performance review. In addition to these short-term uses, we can now use the data collected over many years to better understand the ways in which we have become more successful as well as the areas in which we continue to struggle. Finally, our measurement data has also become an indispensable tool for helping us communicate the nature of our work to donors and board members, helping us to raise more money than ever before.

The Importance of Measurement for Focused Action

The belief that Judaism matters and that it can have a powerful impact on people's lives is something that motivates all of us who are leaders in Jewish organizations. And yet, in all of the challenging business of day-to-day life, we can lose focus on that deeper mission. We get focused on what we have to do each day and not why those actions matters. We are so busy responding to what's urgent, we sometimes fail to do the work that has long-term impact.

One of the ways to stay inspired and to remain focused on the larger mission is to develop solid goals and simple, usable ways to measure success. I am a total convert to the importance of measurement. At first it felt too businesslike to me, but I have seen that once a good system is developed, it can change everything for the better. Part of what is so exhausting about Jewish leadership is that we try to be amazing, for everyone, all the time. When we frame our work that way, it's amorphous and neverending. But when we start to put some numbers and data behind it, our work becomes more concrete. When you know what success looks like, you know when you can go home at night, and you know what to focus on next. I am always surprised at how inspired everyone on our team gets when we review data and see the concrete evidence of what we've accomplished. It is also empowering to learn from the data and gain a deeper understanding of the big picture of our work, as well as the areas in which we need to improve. Perhaps most important of all is the fact that when we find ways to zero in on the most important data, we enable ourselves to play a crucial role in shaping a brighter future for the Jewish people.

Questions for Further Consideration

1. When you think back about your organization over the past year, what kinds of things are you really measuring? What kinds of data inform decision making when it comes to event planning, resource allocation, and staff structure?

2. What would change if your organization inverted the values pyramid?

3. What are the impact goals for some of the most important and successful initiatives and services your organization runs?

4. If there was a clear focus on impact, what initiatives or services might you want to discard because they don't meet your goals?

5. Does your organization have a way of tracking participation in different events, how many people you reach, and how often? If not, what kind of changes would need to be made for your organization to be able to collect that information, enter it into some kind of system (even Excel), and then produce usable reports?

6. If you wanted to begin to measure the impact of different initiatives and leadership opportunities, what might the right surveys look like? Which groups and initiatives would you want to evaluate first?

7

An Educational Philosophy for Impact Organizations

In the last chapter, we talked about how to structure organizations so they can make a big impact on people and help inspire them to live more vibrant Jewish lives. One of the most important ways to do that is through Jewish learning. When it comes to reaching Engagement Jews, Jewish learning stands out as a uniquely powerful tool. In fact, in the case of Hillel, we often find that students who are uninterested in other Jewish opportunities are excited by the chance to learn and deepen their own sense of Jewish authenticity.

> Years ago, I sat down with a group of students to study text together for the first time. They didn't seem excited. Jewish learning evoked memories of tedious nights in Hebrew school or studying for their bar or bat mitzvah ceremony. I began by asking them to tell me what they remembered from the synagogue services of their childhoods. One student said she remembered counting the dust particles floating in the sky that were lit up by sun streaming through the stained glass of the sanctuary. Another student expressed guilt that he never liked services even though he always wanted to feel something. Yet another student said that she loved services. It was a time to think and reflect and

a time when she felt close to her grandparents. Then I passed out a selection from Abraham Joshua Heschel about prayer and synagogues. A lively discussion erupted. Students reflected on what Heschel had to say, on their own thoughts and experiences, as well as on those of their friends in the room. As the teacher, I also began to insert my own perspective, trying to help them see services not as something you go to, but something you participate in. At the end of our discussion, a student named Debbie raised her hand and said, "This conversation was amazing! I always thought that the best way for Hillel to reach new people was to hook them with something fun like a Jewish happy hour and only then trying to connect them to something deeper. But maybe it should be the other way around. Maybe the deeper stuff is really the fun stuff that we should use to hook them."

After all of the different social events and leadership activities that Debbie had participated in over the years, the thing that most excited her was deep Jewish substance. In her short reflection on our learning, Debbie debunked a myth about Jewish engagement that took Hillel professionals decades to understand. There was a long-held belief in Hillel that if we could engage students in something fun and light, like a barbecue, a night of Jewish comedy, or a big party with a lot of Jews, we could then find a way to link them back to some kind of Jewish opportunity with more substance.

It's a great idea in theory, but it never seemed to work. Part of the problem was that we worked so hard building and promoting the big social event that we never had a plan for how to connect the 450 people who showed up and had a great time with the next, more substantial Jewish experience. Another part of the problem with this model is that these kinds of events don't maximize our competitive advantage. You don't need to be Jewish or be a member of a Jewish organization to have a barbecue or go to party. For most Engagement Jews, when they want to do something Jewish, they want it to be something they cannot get anywhere else—and that's where Jewish learning comes in. Helping people to encounter new Jewish ideas is a great way to help them create positive Jewish memories, increase their knowledge, advance their Jewish self-confidence, and feel more connected to other Jews (see figure 5 in chapter 6).

The idea of developing an educational vision is not new, and Hillel didn't invent it, but the process has helped us take our work with students to the next level. Before we invested the time to develop our educational vision, there was no coherency to what we were doing at Penn Hillel. Our staff had widely divergent opinions on how and why to incorporate learning into different initiatives, and there were dozens of weekly student meetings spent entirely on program planning and logistics without any focus on education. We also lacked a shared language about the role of Jewish learning in our work. Finally, it became clear that there were two major types of students, both of whom had major gaps in their Jewish learning that Penn Hillel wasn't adequately addressing. The process of developing an educational vision helped bring all of these factors into greater alignment so that we could focus our strategy and make a bigger impact on students.

I hope you find the ideas as important and inspiring as we do. My goal in sharing them is to provide another tool to focus your own organization's work on something that will make a big difference in people's lives.[1] Regardless of the focus of your particular organization, a good Jewish educational vision can be one of the most powerful ways to reach new Jews and to build a cutting-edge impact organization.

Finding Truth on the Slant

The first step for Penn Hillel was to define the purpose of Jewish learning. Was it to transmit factual information to students so that they become more Jewishly literate? Was it to help them access Jewish wisdom so they felt inspired about their tradition and so that they could live more ethical lives? Or was Jewish learning really just a tool to create community?

We turned to the work of educational philosopher Parker Palmer in thinking about this question.[2] In his book *A Hidden Wholeness*, Palmer shows how a teacher or facilitator can create an environment for exploring the deepest questions any of us ask in life, such as: Does my life matter? Am I loved? What is my role in the world? What parts of myself do I need to change? What parts of myself do I need to accept? As you can imagine, these are the kind of questions that are so deep and so invasive that a discussion leader cannot just dive right in. The "soul is shy," Palmer suggests, and it will hide if it's not approached in the right way. Without trust and safety and a careful approach, people will avoid being vulnerable and honest and will instead keep the discussion safe by dealing with these questions on a more superficial level. The only way to really draw this shy soul out is to approach "on the slant":

> In Western culture, we often seek truth through confrontation. But our headstrong ways of charging at truth scare the shy soul away. If soul truth is to be spoken and heard, it must be approached "on the slant." I do not mean we should be coy, speaking evasively about subjects that make us uncomfortable, which weakens us and our relationships. But soul truth is so powerful that we must allow ourselves to approach it, and it to approach us, indirectly. We must invite, not command, the soul to speak. We must allow, not force, ourselves to listen.[3]

In other words, the best way to help people really learn about and discuss the most important questions in their lives is to approach them carefully and intentionally "on the slant." This means using metaphors in poems, stories, music, or art that embodies that content of the deeper question.[4]

The way this usually happens is that while people are grappling with the text, song, or piece of art, they are really talking about what's happening inside themselves. Almost like a Rorschach test, we see in the art what we need to see in order to better understand and express our own lives. Parents often experience this with children. If you tell your child, "You don't have to be afraid of the dark; there is nothing to be scared of," usually the child won't be able to assimilate the message. But if you tell her a story about someone else who was afraid of the dark until she learned that she was safe and nothing bad would happen, the child will take comfort in the story and how it applies to her. The story helps the child open up and begin to see herself in the story, and she can learn the lesson on the "slant" that might have been hard to learn directly.[5] Palmer calls these stories, poems, and works of art "third things" because they represent neither the voice of the facilitator nor the voice of the participant. They have a voice of their own that tells the truth about a topic through metaphors that allow us to approach the truth on our own terms.[6]

Jewish Learning as a "Third Thing"

Part of the power of studying Jewish texts is that they serve as a "third thing," just like the poetry, songs, and art that Palmer mentions above. Having a discussion about a Jewish text is like having two conversations at once. When we read of the struggles Moses had as a leader, we are reminded of the difficulties we have in our own lives as parents or team leaders. When we discuss a text that asks us to learn from everyone, we are reminded of places in our lives where we have been arrogant and closed off to the ideas of others. In this way, Jewish learning is not just about deepening our Jewish literacy, strengthening our Jewish identity, or learning for its own sake (*Torah lishmah*), it is an invitation to explore our own lives more deeply.

Torah allows us to talk about the most important questions in our lives. As we begin to think, struggle, and reflect together, a classroom becomes one of the safest and most intimate spaces where real community can flourish. On campus we see this all the time. The weekly JRP learning sessions create a totally different space than students find anywhere else in their lives. One fraternity brother told me once, "I don't know how people make it through Penn without something like this. At my fraternity house, all we do is talk about girls, sports, and the stock market. JRP is the place I can go to talk about real things without any of the competition or posturing that goes on in so many other places on campus." My guess is that the same goes for adults, teens, and senior citizens. Wherever we are in our lives, we all need a space free of the petty competitions and daily distractions that can make it hard to really connect with people. Jewish learning can be an antidote for this kind of emotional isolation.

Making Torah Come Alive

Rabbi Dan Smokler

College students and adults are often the most elusive audience for teachers of Torah. They are not coerced into schools where teachers enjoy captive audiences for hours at a time, and they often don't opt in for many of the educational opportunities offered by the Jewish community. And yet, despite these challenges, Hillels around the country are finding ways to reach a larger number of students through Jewish learning opportunities. How can we apply what we are learning on campus to help shape our large efforts to make Jewish learning come to life for all Jews?

A century ago, Franz Rosenzweig sketched a new path for learners to encounter Torah for the first time. He described "a learning in reverse order. A learning that no longer starts from the Torah and leads to life, but the other way round: from life, from a world that knows nothing of the Law, or pretends to know nothing, back to the Torah. That is the sign of the time."[7] Were we to take Rosenzweig's words seriously and begin with "life," we might start with those inchoate, yet pervasive questions that haunt contemporary young Jews: Who am I? What is a good way to live? How can I live meaningfully as an individual in a community? How shall we raise our children? How can I make a positive impact in the world?

We might then humbly suggest that these questions have been taken up by the sages for two millennia, and in learning their approach to our shared questions, we can deepen our own self-understanding. Many of us who teach Torah to emerging adults—in apartments, on campus, at retreats—have learned that the close reading of classical rabbinic texts in the context of an open-ended inquiry into life's great questions can become one of the rare places in life where such are surfaced explicitly. I have seen sorority girls debate the virtues of a true friend while studying Talmud together. I have seen young singles struggle to articulate the meaning of intimacy in their lives while parsing a midrash. For the young person who has yet to marry, to decide where to raise children, or to settle in a career, the stakes of adjudicating these and other questions are high.

I would suggest that we must extend this kind of learning to older adults as well. For the young person, choosing how to live is always hard, but when life unfolds in an open, fluid society replete with ever-new dazzling possibilities of choice, deciding how we should live becomes a lifelong struggle with persistent, unresolved questions. Thus we might imagine how to extend the Torah of young adults—its style, form, and content—which is being worked out, teacher by teacher, to the rest of the broader community. In so doing, we might find, collectively, as Rosenzweig says, a pathway back into "the heart of life."

Is Truth-Seeking Enough? Mapping the Sweet Spot for Jewish Learning

As inspiring as Palmer's ideas were for the staff at Penn Hillel, we also knew that something else was needed. Jewish learning couldn't just be about deep community and seeking truth on the slant, it also had to be about content, information, and Jewish confidence.[8] The stories of Isaac and Paige tell this story in a powerful way:

> Isaac was an Orthodox student who grew up in Teaneck. He went to yeshiva, loved summer camp, and spent a gap year in Israel studying Torah all day and night. When he got to Penn, he had an air of confidence and competence about him. He was smart, he could speak Hebrew like an Israeli, he could read and understand almost any Jewish text in the original, and he could lead services and read Torah in a way that was both skillful and beautiful. Soon after he arrived at Penn, he had a bit of a Jewish crisis. Up until that point in his life, he had lived only in Orthodox communities. All of a sudden he was encountering new ideas and new ways of relating to Judaism that excited him. He was loving his academic Bible class even though it contradicted many of the ideas he learned at yeshiva. He was getting to know all sorts of secular Jews and people from different religious traditions. He realized that he came from a narrow world, and he was shocked to find how much he liked the larger world. While he still loved traditional Judaism, his perspective was changing, and he wanted to live in a more diverse world. But how? What did his traditional approach to Judaism mean with all of this new information? Isaac really struggled to find a way to make sense of how he could both own the Judaism he grew up with and assimilate all of the new possibilities presented by the larger secular world surrounding him.

Paige, on the other hand, grew up in a secular environment. She had a Reform bat mitzvah ceremony, but now she considers herself "just Jewish." Although she isn't Jewishly active, she feels proud of her Judaism. For her, it's all about making the world a better place and becoming a better person. Growing up, at Hanukkah time her family would donate toys to children who were less fortunate, and on Passover, while they may not have read the whole Haggadah, they did take time to discuss how they had an obligation to "free others" who are oppressed today, because they were slaves in Egypt centuries ago. One of the reasons she isn't more "involved" in Jewish life is that she isn't comfortable in formal Jewish spaces and therefore avoids them. She doesn't feel like she knows enough. Anything in Hebrew is really intimidating because she can barely sound out the words. This tendency followed Paige to college, where she encountered so many Jews like Isaac—people who "knew everything" and who made her feel even more insecure and inauthentic about her Judaism.

Hundreds of other Jewish students and adults live out their own versions of this same story every day. If you grew up in the liberal denominations of Judaism like Paige, you may feel like you have well-developed abilities to think about the meaning of Judaism and how to extract universal messages from Jewish texts and rituals. If you grew up more traditional like Isaac did, you might have an abundance of tools for Jewish living, but still struggle to find the meaning in Judaism outside of observance.

After listening to hundreds of stories from different students just like Isaac and Paige, we learned that what people knew about Judaism and how they processed that information had a huge impact on their excitement levels about Jewish life. If people felt that Judaism either had no meaning or was inaccessible, all other forms of Jewish expression were muted. Therefore, part of our approach to Jewish engagement is to help our students find deeper meaning and new access points in Jewish life. We also learned that Jewish learning had to serve multiple roles at one time. It couldn't just be about meaning making and big universal questions that applied to everyone, nor could it just be about content transmission and particularistic topics that applied only to Jews. For Hillel to achieve its mission, we would need to implement Jewish learning that could do both things simultaneously.

So how did we do this? The first step was to look even deeper into what was really happening in each and every learning environment. In doing so, we realized that in order to create the most effective educational philosophy, we had to acknowledge that there are three voices present in every educational setting and that all three need to be honored, addressed, and amplified. Those voices belong to the teacher, the student, and the subject (in many cases a Torah text).[9] Allowing all three to speak naturally creates balance between the universal and the particular, and between transmission of content and meaning making. In practical terms this means the teacher cannot just facilitate a "feel good" conversation that only gives voice to what the students already feel; he or she needs to have a compelling and authentic perspective that can be used to challenge the ideas of the students and the text. The student's job is more than just to submit to the power of the text or the teacher. His or her feelings, experience, wisdom, and thoughts are essential to the process as well.

While this sounds easy to achieve, in looking at our work in Hillel and in other informal Jewish educational spaces, we saw a different reality. When it came to non-Orthodox Jewish learning, more often than not, the voice of the teacher and the text were largely absent. The teacher would offer a text to start the conversation, and the rest of the time would be spent addressing students' reactions and feelings without ever devoting time to really understanding the perspective of the text or the teacher.[10] While this kind of discussion is great for building community, it's less than ideal for actually helping students learn. Without the external voices of the Jewish sources and the facilitators, there is nothing present to challenge students to think beyond their own experiences and perspectives.

Rabbi Josh Bolton (the senior Jewish educator at Penn Hillel) and I used to have long conversations about what this really looked like in real life and how we could get other people in the organization to join this conversation about creating Jewish learning experiences that balanced all of these things. Figure 6 is the more polished version of something I

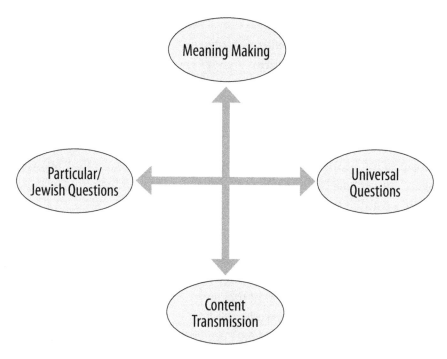

Figure 6. The four quadrants of Jewish learning

scribbled on a piece of scratch paper at the end of one of those conversations. It has become the basis for how we talk to staff, students, and donors about Penn Hillel's educational vision.

You'll notice that there are two axes: The vertical one goes from "meaning making" to "content transmission"—the difference between a class discussion that gives space to reflect on how the themes of a Jewish holiday can apply to our lives today and a class that is focused on giving students the information to understand the history of how that holiday developed. The horizontal axis goes from topics that are particular to Judaism to topics that are about universal life questions—this is the difference between a class about whether Jews eat legumes (*kitniyot*) on Passover versus a discussion about what it means to be a true friend.

In much of our work, the goal is that each class or larger educational initiative should be designed and taught so that it can operate effectively in each of the four quadrants: it would provoke students to contemplate big, universal questions that offer meaningful and practical wisdom that they could use in their daily lives while at the same time transmitting enough

Jewish content to reinforce their connection to Judaism and to make them more confident and inspired Jewish citizens.

That said, not every learning experience at Penn Hillel works that way. There are certainly times when people just need a space to process and think without the need to learn new information. The inverse is true as well. Sometime a great lecture on the current state of Israeli politics is exactly what a student needs. The goal in our using this chart is to help our organization be smarter and more intentional in how we create a balanced set of educational opportunities. To make this idea come to life, I want to share a real-life example with you.

> I was teaching a class on prayer for JRP years ago, and the topic of class was the *Shema*. My goal in the conversation was to hit all four quadrants: I wanted the students to learn new information, to make meaning out of the prayer, and to deal with it on both a particular and universal level.
>
> I started by asking the group to reflect on when and where they feel close to God. Students had a lot to say. Some talked about feeling close to God in nature, some felt that God was there during difficult times, and some admitted that they never felt close to God. Then I handed out a copy of the *Shema* prayer, broke them into pairs (*chevrutas*), and asked them to focus on the first and most famous phrase— "Hear O Israel, Adonai is our God, Adonai is One"—and try to figure out what it teaches us about God. After a brief discussion, most students related the same types of answers: the *Shema* teaches us that we believe in only one God rather than many gods. Of course while this is a correct answer, I wanted to push them further than what they had already learned in Hebrew school. So I passed out a Hasidic text that asserted that God is not just in heaven, but everywhere— in the beauty of nature, in the words of great poets, and in the artistic creations of great artists. After the students read and discussed the text, I explained that it was expressing a concept called Hasidic immanentism. I gave them some more historical context to help them better understand who the author of the text was and the real meaning of Hasidic Judaism (most of them

assumed it just meant ultra-Orthodox). We spent the final part of the conversation going back to the text of the *Shema* and exploring what happens when you read it through the lens of Hasidic immanentism. Rather than just understanding "God is One" as referring to monotheism, now all of a sudden once the prayer means that God is in everything, new layers of spiritual and ethical meaning emerge. Students started to riff on the possible ways to understand this. A young woman said, "If the *Shema* reminds us that God is in everything and everyone, that explains why we feel so connected to other people; we can sense that God is in them too." Another student added, "That means that the *Shema* prayer is really about ethics then. If God is in everyone, that means that every time we hurt someone, every time we make someone feel small, we are actually diminishing God's oneness in the world." From here the discussion kept going to even include interpretations of the *Shema* as an environmental prayer—if God is in everything, anything we do to destroy the planet also lessens God in the world.

"I may not be able to see it right now, but the Holy One fills all creation, being is made of God, you and I, everything is made of God—even the grains of sand beneath my feet, the whole world is included."

—Rabbi Kalonymous Kalman Shapira of Piesetzna

You can see that this class was playing on many different levels at the same time. When students learned more about the *Shema* and Hasidic Judaism, there was content transmission. When students started to offer their own interpretations of what the prayer meant in their lives, there was meaning making. When students used the new ways of understanding the *Shema* and Hasidic thought to reinterpret what Judaism means to them, they were operating on a level of Jewish particularism. And when they proceeded to offer ethical and environmental interpretations of these ideas, they were operating on a universal level. This is just one example, but I hope that it sparks your imagination about the different ways to apply this kind of educational philosophy to the work of your own organization.

From Classes to Communities

The final shift we made as Penn Hillel continued to develops its educational vision was a shift from thinking about classes to a focus on building learning communities. We found that by increasing the strength of the community among the learners, we could dramatically increase the impact of the learning. Unlike a traditional class, creating a learning community required a deep and intentional focus. The community created a different kind of intimacy among its members. We wanted students to do more than learn something new; we wanted them to make new friends and to be able to explore life's deepest questions. We try to create community in any way we can. Sometimes it happens through simple things like making sure people know each other's names and a bit about their Jewish story. Sometimes, it means saving time for group discussions and for *chevruta* (paired) learning. Sometimes it's about making sure that students can have dinner together and get to know each other; nothing builds culture and community like food. Finally, our best educational experiences include some kind of retreat or immersive experience that allows the students to go away together to build the kind of personal connections that can only happen away from all the distractions of daily life.

Rabbi Shimon bar Yochai says: "This is like a person who brought two ships and anchored them together and placed them in the middle of the sea and built upon them a palace. As long as the ships are tied to each other—the palace exists. Once the ships separate from each other—the palace cannot exist."

—*Sifre* on Deuteronomy

Another shift is more counterintuitive. We moved from a model of low boundaries to one of high boundaries.[11] In its early days, JRP's goal was to make Jewish learning easy, cool, and accessible without requiring any kind of commitment from the students. We would host "Torah on Tap" at a local bar and would spread the word among students on campus by "talking it up," saying things like, "We're doing a Torah on Tap later this week. It should be cool. Just stop by if you're interested." More often than not, though, these educational initiatives were lose-lose situations.

Torah study, even in a bar, is ultimately not all that "cool," and how deeply inspiring can you really be in a noisy pub for an audience who have already had a few drinks? But the biggest problem with this kind of event is that even though they were supposed to be fun and easily accessible, very few students came, and those who did were the ones who were already connected to Jewish life. There was something about the way we were promoting these events that just wasn't working.

After years of experimenting with these kinds of education initiatives, we tried taking a totally different approach. Rather than trying to lower the boundaries, we raised them. Rather than making Jewish learning casual, we made it special. Rather than inviting a huge number of people to "stop by if they could," we tapped a few people to apply to specialized programs. We added an application process with an interview where we talked directly about the nature of the commitment to this learning initiative. It wasn't open to everyone. We didn't want to be exclusive, but we wanted the experiences to be customized. Each learning opportunity was specially formulated to bring together a particular type of Jewish student with a particular set of Jewish questions. Instead of trying to be cool, we decided to be deep.

What happened next surprised us. The numbers of people who applied and wanted to commit to the more serious educational initiative were much higher than t he numbers of people who ever showed up to the "cool" one-off program. We also found that because we were intentionally tapping people to apply, Hillel was better able to reach students from all different Jewish backgrounds rather than just those who were already self-motivated to seek out Jewish life. Students were turned on by how seriously we took it, because their own Jewish questions and insecurities felt serious to them. The commitment in many ways lowered the social risk of joining. When it was a casual "stop by if you can," students never knew who would be there and if they would feel comfortable. Once we tapped them and could explain that the initiative was designed for people just like them, they had a better sense that they would fit in. Also, because each learning community lasted for several weeks, there was a better chance they would actually get to know the other people in the group.

Not only did creating higher boundaries help Penn Hillel increase the levels of interest and commitment from students, but we also learned that in a casual, one-off, learning event, it was very hard to inspire substantive content and conversation. The depth took time. Both the group and the teacher needed time to get to know one another.

Making an Impact Through Jewish Learning

We know from the data that Jews today report having intensely positive feelings about being Jewish. They want to learn more about Judaism, they want to connect deeply with other Jews, and they want to feel more authentic and confident in their own Jewish identity. That's why building organizations that are focused on impact and that have a deep educational philosophy are some of our best tools to engage new populations of Jews.

Questions for Further Consideration

1. Does your organization have a conscious and intentional educational philosophy?

2. Do you have a shared language for Jewish education that can help your professional and volunteer leaders plan, envision, and create more opportunities for transformative Jewish experiences?

3. Where and when does Jewish learning take place in your organization?

4. Looking back at the diagram of the four quadrants of Jewish learning (figure 6):

   a. When you think about your professional leaders, in which spaces are they most effective?

   b. When you think about your constituency, which quadrants are most important and relevant for them? Which are least?

   c. When you map out the various opportunities that exist for Jewish learning, to what degree do they touch all four quadrants?

5. What types of Jewish information, ideas, values, and resources could help inspire Jewish growth for the people connected to your organization?

8

Asset-Based Community Development Theory

So far we have used methodologies and examples from both the business world and Penn Hillel to explore new ways that Jewish organizations can reinvent themselves. Now I want to share with you a model that comes from a different discipline. The idea of "asset-based community development" was originally conceptualized by Northwestern University professors John McKnight and John Kretzmann to help guide their work in healing America's inner cities. The basic premise is that when communities are in decline, leadership often gets stuck in what they call "deficiency-based community development" thinking. This strategy begins with the assumption that the best way to help a community in need is to figure how to fix its problems. Focusing on what is wrong leads to a whole set of unintended negative consequences.[1] Instead, if communities were to start by focusing on what's working and by building on their assets, organizations could actually do a dramatically better job of fulfilling their mission.

I want to look at this process in two steps: first by exploring the harm that deficiency thinking can have, and then by exploring how an asset-based approach can be truly transformative. Take, for example, the following story from Penn Hillel:

One December we learned that the International Boycott Divestment and Sanctions (BDS) movement would be hosting their international conference at Penn the following spring. As you can imagine, this was not taken lightly. Jewish leaders from across campus and all over North America rushed into action to help Penn Hillel respond to this anti-Israel conference. Immediately we began to discuss our plan of action: we were to educate students about BDS, create a counter-conference to refute false claims made by BDS speakers, protect students from hateful propaganda, and stop the spread of false and harmful BDS information. We were on fire. We felt a tremendous need to control the situation and regain any power that might be lost by the presence of BDS on campus. But something about this counter-campaign felt wrong.

During one late-night strategy-session with students, I remembered asset-based community development theory. I shared the idea with students. What if, rather than reacting and trying to fix the problems created by the BDS conference, we instead used it as an opportunity to build on the community's assets and to inspire hundreds of students to feel more connected to Israel? Something about the idea of starting with the positive and building on existing assets felt right.

The shift in thinking was a game changer, and it led to a totally different kind of strategy. We looked at the numbers. Maybe a dozen students out of 10,000 undergraduates were active with BDS, while Hillel had close to 650 students working in some kind of leadership position and nearly 250 student leaders working as pro-Israel activists on campus. Once we saw the assets, we realized that BDS wasn't a threat we had to fight—they were too small and insignificant. In reality, this anti-Israel conference was an opportunity. Penn Hillel had other assets too: access to a wide array of social networks on campus that ran through every student interest group; great skill creating deep educational experiences and past success facilitating meaningful conversations about difficult topics; and a nationwide network of alumni and parents who could help support the great ideas students would come up with. Then we looked at our mission statement and reminded ourselves that Hillel's goal was not to defeat BDS—the goal was to deepen students' connection to Israel and to Judaism. The conference would come and go in a weekend, but a deep connection with Israel would last a lifetime.

From then on, we focused on building on our strengths and trying to push the idea of "fixing problems" aside. In the end, we created a weekend-long series of opportunities for students to learn more about and get more connected with Israel. We invited Professor Alan Dershowitz to speak before a sold-out auditorium of nearly 900 people. We worked with leaders in different fraternities and sororities to throw an "Invest in Israel Party" for over 300 students, which raised $7,000 for an Israeli charity. We facilitated the creation of a leadership statement in support of Israel, signed by over 57 different leaders representing student groups ranging from the Penn Democrats to the College Republicans to the Penn basketball team. We also created an initiative call "Israel Across Penn," where 48 different students hosted Shabbat dinners and led their own positive discussions about Israel, which engaged over 800 Jewish and non-Jewish students. Not only did these different projects reach over 1,400 students, but all of the different initiatives, in their own way, hit their impact goals of helping students feel inspired about Israel.

It turned out that the BDS conference was quiet and uneventful. While some students attended, most of the people who participated were from outside the university community. Meanwhile, over 1,400 students had the opportunity to connect more deeply with Israel. After all of the tumult of the conference passed, we saw the fruits of our labors. Students were energized and inspired. The number of students active in all of the pro-Israel groups on campus grew. Birthright Israel registration increased.

While this story is one dramatic example, the power of starting with what's right rather than what's wrong is an idea that has powerful applications for so much of the work we do as Jewish leaders.

What's wrong about starting with what's wrong

Many Jewish organizations rely on deficiency-based thinking, which creates a seemingly endless list of things that are going wrong. This deeply held set of assumptions and fears about the problems facing the community is called a deficiency or needs map.[2]

Figure 7 is an example of what the deficiency map for a Jewish community might look like. Issues like assimilation, low levels of affiliation, and anti-Israel sentiment form a core set of fears and concerns that Jews have about the health of their communities. Our concerns for these deficiencies not only consume a tremendous amount of time, energy, and money, they also shape the way that we understand the current state of Jewish life and affect how organizations set their priorities.

Organizations that get stuck in a deficiency-based approach succumb to six basic faults. Focusing on what's wrong and what needs to be fixed forces professional and volunteer leaders into a reactionary posture. From there, everything from strategic planning to resource allocation is

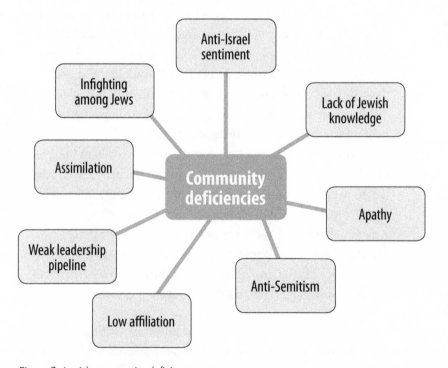

Figure 7. Jewish community deficiency map

informed by the goal of organizational survival rather than transformation. This in turn leads to big, slow institutions made up of layers of committees and different leadership groups who must participate in decision making, thereby slowing down the organization's ability to respond the community in real time. The top level of leadership retains the main resources and skills, which keeps those very things from the people who need it most—community members. Once the power is out of their hands, the people in the community are forced into a passive, "client" position, while the organizations function like a service provider—community members can choose to make use of the organization's programs or services or not, but they are not given the tools of self-empowerment. Finally, because they now feel like clients rather than partners, they see no need to work together to solve their own problems. In this way, the organization actually contributes to lower levels of connectedness among community members.[3]

Figure 8 illustrates what this phenomenon looks like. The center is filled by a large, centralized organization that traps resources, money, and power within the institution.[4] It is run by professionals and experts who envision, create, and deliver the programs and services that are needed by the community.[5] For an institution like this to remain relevant and well-funded, it needs to maintain some ownership and control over the programs. Even though the organizational leaders speak publicly about the value of community, the institution itself tends to undermine that community. The diagram depicts an organization replacing real community with individual client relationships. Rather than community members relating to one another and self-organizing to address their own problems and needs, they turn to the central body to receive the services they need.

When the "passive client" model becomes the primary lens through which an organization views the community it serves, a cascade of consequences follows. Any crisis forces the organization to respond with programs and services for the community. The more programs and services created, the more the community comes to rely on them and the more the organization perceives itself as relevant and successful.[6] The rabbi serves as the expert who teaches Torah and officiates at services and life-cycle events. The cantor is the professional musician and singer who can lead services. A trained Jewish educator is responsible for educating our

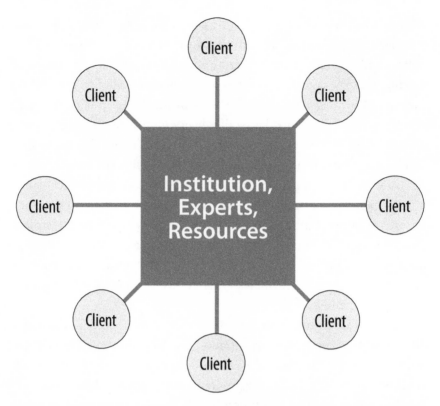

Figure 8. Centralized organization. This is what organizations tend to look like when they do deficiency-based community development.

children. In each of these situations, responsibility for Jewish life is taken away from the individual or the family and is transferred to a professional "expert." Jewish life is no longer something that happens at home around the dinner table; it is something that requires membership and a building. Organizing the Jewish community in this way reinforces a kind of segmentation whereby a person who wants to participate in something Jewish must leave behind their "normal life" and travel to some Jewish place where real "Jewish life" happens.

"And you shall teach your children, speaking of [these words] when you sit at home and when you are on the way."
—*Shema* prayer
(Deuteronomy 6:7)

The story of a former JRP student intern at Penn Hillel highlights just how deeply held this form of segmentation can be:

While on campus, Samantha was the poster child for the positive impact that JRP could have on students. Previously, she had never been part of a Jewish community. She had very few Jewish friends, and the ones she did have never explored Judaism with each other. At Penn, JRP engaged her deeply by creating opportunities for Jewish learning and by empowering her to create Jewish experiences for people in her social network (e.g., Shabbat dinners, Jewish conversations), all of which were outside the framework of Hillel and the institutional Jewish community. A few years later, Samantha claimed that she no longer "did anything Jewish." She explained that she didn't go to synagogue or Jewish young professional events. Interestingly, even though her whole experience with JRP was meant to bolster her Jewish identity in the world at large, she still equated Jewish life with physical institutions. Samantha's sense of segmentation was so strong that she didn't even realize the ways in which she was actively Jewish—she had started to read Jewish books in her spare time; she had more Jewish friends than ever before; and she started to go to different Shabbat dinners around the city with some regularity—and yet she felt inactive.

Samantha is not alone in discounting the value of the Jewish activities enacted outside of Jewish institutional spaces. Organizational leaders often make the same mistake and assume that just because someone is not "showing up" or "affiliating" it also means they are not living a vibrant and satisfying Jewish life. This kind of assumption undervalues and ignores a whole array of positive Jewish activity that is self-initiated by and deeply meaningful for millions of Jews.[7] More than that, when we assume that the only Jewish activities that count are the ones that take place in our buildings, we create an impossible set of expectations for Jewish organizations. One or two clergy in a synagogue could never have enough time, let alone the emotional, spiritual, and intellectual range, to meet the needs of a congregation of some seven hundred family units. When the professionals and leaders try to do it all, they end up feeling overstretched and burned out, while many community members still feel underserved.

This model of assuming that an institution can provide everything is not sustainable. Even if it were, it's not even ideal. Think about the most important and meaningful Jewish moments of learning, ritual, and community service in your own life. How many of them have taken place in small groups with family and friends and not in a formal context? My guess is that part of what was so special about these experiences is that you were involved in creating them and they took place on your own terms—something that is hard for institutions to replicate. So for Jewish organizations to more fully achieve their missions, they need more than a class of professional leaders to serve as creators of Jewish life. They also need a strategy for helping communities unlock the power of individuals and social networks in order to dramatically expand the number of people who can serve as creators of Jewish life alongside the professionals. As the next section will show, the key to achieving this is to shift our focus from fixing what's wrong to building upon what's right.

What's Right About Starting with What's Right

We all know that a strategy that only focuses on what's wrong doesn't work. No one wants to board a sinking ship. The constant crisis narrative can be a real turnoff to young, talented people who are not already committed to battling all that is wrong in the community. As Woody Allen put it, "For Jews, swimming is not drowning." And yet, as Richard Joel, former president of Hillel International, often noted, "For younger Jews today, not drowning is not enough." Jews in America have more freedom and choice about how they understand and construct their identity and community than at any other time in Jewish history. If the Jewish community wants to attract the best and brightest, Judaism needs to have a positive value proposition that offers more than survival.

What would happen if we started with the positive? In the Jewish community, rather than starting with assimilation, apathy, and low level of affiliation, we can start our strategic thinking with what works and what is available. For example, an asset map of the Jewish community might look something like figure 9. Each box in this cluster represents a different asset that can serve the community and build a stronger organization. Features of the community like affluence, concentration of

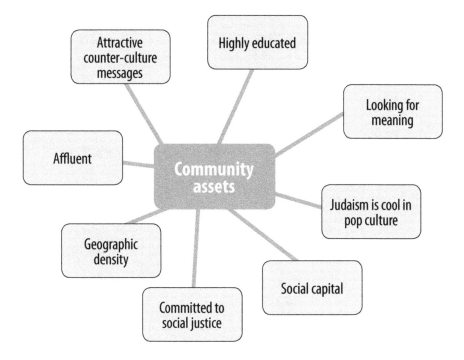

Figure 9. Jewish community asset map

population in a particular geographic area, and a deep commitment to education highlight areas of commonality. The fact that many Jews are committed to social justice and are looking for meaning in their lives and in their religion and that Judaism is highly regarded in pop culture creates opportunities for programmatic engagement.

An organization that stays focused on what's right ends up taking on the following five characteristics:

> "[In order to transform yourself] you must search and search until you find some good point inside yourself to give you new life and make you happy. Through this you will be able to come back to God."
> —Rebbe Nachman of Breslov

1. Focus is on assets rather than deficiencies.
2. Transformation is the goal, not survival.
3. Organizations become smaller and faster moving.

4. Resources are no longer trapped in the institution; instead they get to the people who need them in a way that fosters real community and partnerships.

5. Focus is on the well-being of individuals in the community rather than the institution.[8]

When asset-based community development is done well, it transforms the way that organizations look and act. It also dramatically expands the power of an organization to do a better job of fulfilling its mission even without the addition of new financial resources. Figure 10 , based on Clay Shirky's excellent work in *Here Comes Everybody: The Power of Organizing Without Organizations*, illustrates these changes. The large square in the center represents the community organization. The dots located on

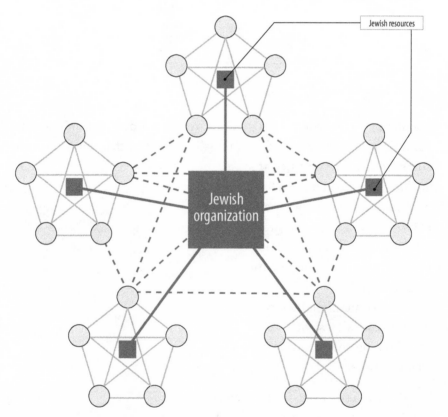

Figure 10. Networked organization. This is what organizations tend to look like when they do asset-based community development. Note the tightly networked clusters outside the organization.

the outside of each cluster represent people living in that community, and the lines indicate their connection to each other and the organization. The smaller squares located inside each cluster represent the ways in which the organization is able to deliver Jewish resources, tools, and support to each group of people, empowering them to create Jewish life for themselves.

Rather than having a large, centralized organization that holds all of the power, resources, and expertise so that it can deliver services to an array of individual passive clients (as seen in the deficiency-based approach in figure 8), the model of the asset-based approach depicted in figure 10 shows a smaller, more nimble organization at the center.

"The greatest level, above which there is no greater, is to support a fellow Jew by endowing him with a gift or a loan, or entering into a partnership with him, or finding employment for him, in order to strengthen his hand until he need no longer be in dependence upon others."

—Maimonides

Rather than focusing on institutional needs and constantly trying to grow itself, the organization has shifted its focus to the needs of the community. In this model, the organization succeeds in delivering resources directly to people where they are.

The way that the individuals relate to the organization is also different in the asset-based model. Rather than having each individual relate to the organization directly as a separate client, in this diagram people also relate to one another and form micro-communities. A micro-community is a term used by social scientists to refer to a small subset of the population, in contradistinction to a macro-community. For the purposes of this book, the term "micro-community" refers to smaller-group experiences and social networks. Imagine something more like a book club than a large High Holy Day service.

The way that success is measured is also entirely different. In a deficiency-based approach, success is based on the size of the central organization in the middle (think annual budget) and the number of clients served (think membership or programmatic participation). In an asset-based approach, success is measured in much more complex ways, through five categories:

1. **Quantity:** The amount of positive Jewish activity taking place (how many squares there are), the number of clusters that exist, and the number of people in each cluster.
2. **Quality:** The depth, power, and vibrancy of the Jewish experiences. In a realistic map, some squares may represent light touches, while others may represent transformative Jewish experiences.
3. **Empowerment:** The ability of the organization to deliver Jewish tools that foster a sense of empowerment, rather than a sense of dependence.
4. **Connectivity:** The interconnectedness of each cluster. The more densely connected each cluster is within itself demonstrates the strength of the micro-community. The interconnectedness of different clusters to each other demonstrates the strength of the macro-community.
5. **Permeability:** The degree of ease with which individuals can join a cluster and move from one cluster to another. The organization should take steps to reward this permeability and use best practices of "network weaving," the practice of consciously and strategically nurturing the mixing of people who belong to different social networks,[9] to ensure this social mobility can take place. Permeability also measures how open and welcoming a community is and ensures that it avoids the trap of being cliquey.

Defining Our Terms: What Assets Really Matter?

Now that we know the importance of starting with the "good news" and building from there, we need to define the types of assets that we can build on.

Asset #1: Social Capital

In his best-selling book *The Tipping Point*, Malcolm Gladwell defines three basic types of influential people in communities: connectors, salesmen, and mavens. Together, these are the people who possess a certain social power, who can affect behavior, inspire others to action, and connect people with each other.[10] Connectors are network weavers—they bring together the various social groups to whom they have deep connections and act as social bridges between them. Salesmen are trendsetters who directly affect others by promoting new products or programs. Mavens are the people in your community who seem to always know everything about everything.

Asset #2: Geographic Capital

Knowing where people in the community tend to gather, such as community centers, parks, coffee shops, and clubs, are ways of mapping geographic capital. For Jewish organizations, simply knowing where their members live provides a wealth of potential opportunity for engagement work. Not only does creating an asset map of geographic locations help us to literally find constituents where they live, work, and play, it also helps us understand the demographics of our community at large and builds on our use of social capital. When we know where various connectors, salesmen, and mavens live their lives, we can better use those relationships to further expand the opportunities for Jewish experience.

The trick here is to avoid the trap of immediately moving toward the creation of new programs and services, but rather "to locate all of the available local assets, to begin connecting them with one another in ways that multiply their power and effectiveness."[11] In other words, the mapping itself does not tell you how to regenerate the community. Rather, once a community succeeds in mapping their assets in a nuanced way, it reveals the next set of relationships to be created. Eventually, through the building of these relationships, a new set of opportunities for Jewish life will be created in which individuals become partners and co-creators rather than passive clients.

Using Technology to Map Jewish Populations
Rabbi Josh Heller

One of the classic texts of the biblical tradition describes God reaching out to save Ishmael *ba'asher hu sham*, "where he was at that moment" (Genesis 21:17). We can read the text idiomatically, to refer to Ishmael's spiritual state, or we can take it literally, to indicate that God noted the physical place where Ishmael was, and that that truly mattered.

Today, we tend to downplay physical proximity in favor of virtual and social media connections. Indeed, some research has shown that people are less connected to their neighbors than they once were.[12] However, closer examination reveals that physical location still matters just as much as it ever did in creating engaged community networks. Technological tools for geolocation (finding the physical location of our constituents) can help us understand and maximize the impact of physical location on the networks of Jews that we seek to engage.

The simplest approach is to categorize constituents by zip code. It is relatively easy, with a congregant database or spread-sheet that includes address, age, and date joined, to determine a tremendous amount about where one's community "is." How many families live in a particular area? What's the average age or number of children for those families?

However, for many of us, columns of raw numbers on a spreadsheet are hard to interpret. As the rabbi of Congrega-tion B'nai Torah, a suburban congregation outside of Atlanta, I developed and adapted techniques to visualize the data graph-ically, so that our decision makers could better understand where our congregants lived. Seeing a color map has a much greater impact than trying to interpret a column of numbers. While at one time more specialized technology was needed, as of this writing most of the functionality can be obtained using the map creation functions of Google Maps.[13]

We dump our membership data into text/csv format and upload it into a "private" but shareable map. Each family's home appears on a map that can be zoomed or shared. We can color code dots based on age, length of membership, or any other relevant data that we maintain.

With our hundreds of families displayed visually, patterns immediately jumped out at us. We quickly realized that a zip code several miles away included many of our youngest and newest members, and we began targeting activities in that area to engage those members and their friends. We found that our congregants in another area were primarily longtime members who were empty nesters, and we could think about ways to create a stronger sense of community for them.

Over time, we also found that our congregation could use location-based analysis of our constituents to solve many day-to-day problems. We had better information about who to call to help with an out-of-the-way shivah minyan. When elderly congregants needed a ride to services, it was easy to see whose route to synagogue passed by their residence. When we needed to identify a family to help host Shabbat guests for an event at a different synagogue several miles away, we could immediately see who lived within a one-mile radius. That conversation prompted me to think more deeply about those congregants who were driving past one or more other congregations to come to us. Could we offer something that would give them reason to continue to come, or was it in everyone's best interest for them to find a synagogue where they could be engaged more easily?

What questions might your community answer using geolocation tools? Would you be better able to create events at local venues or private homes or to establish neighborhood *chavurot*, to strengthen local affinity? Could you suggest carpool routes or ride-share locations? Correlate zip code data with home values from a real estate website, to assess donor capacity? Would a strategic analysis show that your facility or typical sites for activities are in the best possible location to serve your target populations?

Asset #3: Community Partners

Community partners are those organizations that operate in overlapping circles with yours, such as local charities, churches, mosques, YMCAs, cultural or educational institutions, and social clubs. With this asset, the key is to find the people within those organizations with whom you already have existing relationships, so that those people can bridge the gap between the two communities.

When this is done successfully, it creates an opportunity for your organization to meet and engage new people, to rebrand itself as more diverse and inclusive, and to find new cost-saving ways of sharing resources.[14]

This methodology can also be applied to community partnerships within the Jewish world as well. For example, in northern New Jersey, Jewish organizations are banding together with the help of the local Federation to collectively negotiate discounts on everything from electricity to landscaping services. Once the leadership was able to get the heads of the various organizations to see their counterparts as partners and not as competitors, the community was able to save millions of dollars simply by cooperating on things that were mutually beneficial to everyone.[15] Similarly, some synagogues facing large infrastructures with diminishing memberships are working together to join forces, share space, and lessen the financial burdens that hold back their individual organizations.[16]

A Practical Guide to Moving Forward

What does it take to move from the deficiency-based approach to a model that focuses on available assets? And what would a successful shift look like on the ground? To make these changes a reality, there are five key strategies that can help: shifting from macro- to micro-communities,[17] moving out of a physical space, making use of asset mapping, increasing the number of "owners," and shifting from a model of service provider to that of empowering others.

Strategy #1: Shift from Macro-Communities to Micro-Communities

Shifting from macro-communities to micro-communities means placing at least as much value on the number of congregants having Shabbat dinners together each week in small groups as the number of people who show up at High Holy Day services or other large events throughout the year. It's all about finding ways to use micro-community events to balance out the macro-community events.

The major objection to this shift is the feeling that something sacred will be lost if we focus on small communities and not large ones. There is something powerful about having the whole congregation together at certain times throughout the year, and people want to feel connected to a larger sense of community. A focus on micro-communities, however, need not eliminate this larger communal feeling. The classic example of this is the Passover seder. Small groups of families and friends perform this ritual in homes all over the world, and even though the whole Jewish community is not together in one room, there is a strong sense of collective action.

Strategy #2: Get Out of the Building

No Jewish organization, whether it is a synagogue, Hillel, JCC, or day school, should rely solely upon a central, physical structure to house all official Jewish life. Buildings can, and should, play an important functional and symbolic role, but they should not be used as a crutch. To unlock various social and geographic assets and to really engage post-institutional Jews, Jewish life needs to take place in the same places where people live their lives.[18] This minimizes barriers to involvement and reduces the sense of segmentation between "real life" and "Jewish life." When an asset-based approach takes its fullest form, it supplements the usual building-based Jewish opportunities with other Jewish experiences that are peer-led and that take place outside of formal Jewish spaces. These additional entry points into Jewish life not only help your organization dramatically increase the number of people it engages, but because you have removed barriers to "involvement," it will also expand the diversity of people you reach.

Strategy #3: Make Use of Asset Mapping

To achieve an organization that can really reach Engagement Jews, the leadership needs to map and activate different social connectors and influencers in every possible area. Without activating these relationships and empowering these micro-communities to create Jewish life for themselves, it is nearly impossible to overcome the "passive client model." The exercise of mapping your assets will help you figure out who is out there and who can help. The next step is to then go and build relationships with them. Chapter 9 will delve into the art of transforming these new contacts into active creators of Jewish life and partners in your mission.

Strategy #4: Dramatically Increase the Number of Owners

To really transform your organization's ability to reach new people, it needs to dramatically increase and diversify the number of people who feel ownership of the programmatic offerings created. While it is always important to increase the diversity of the board and the size of a planning committee for an event geared toward macro-community, the goal here is different. This model creates a new kind of leadership and peer owner-ship that exists outside the boundaries of the organizational framework and without a title. It is about empowering Jews who live in the commu-nity to organize their social networks and create Jewish life experiences that emerge organically from the needs, interests, and social connections already available. For this to work, leadership must cede centralized con-trol and trust the wisdom of communities.

Strategy #5: Shift from Providing to Empowering

The paradigm and terminology around leadership also have to change for both professionals and volunteers alike. When it comes to profes-sional leadership like rabbis, cantors, and educators, the role must shift from "experts performing functions" to "facilitators empowering and inspiring others to act." Again, this does not mean that there is no role for experts to practice their craft. The community will always need gifted teachers, pastoral care providers, musicians, and spiritual lead-ers. Rather, in this new model, professional leadership and the organiza-tions they serve also need to supplement their talents with the talents of others.

In terms of lay leadership, a shift must also occur. Currently, volunteer leadership in the Jewish community is a euphemism for one of two things: (1) donating money and/or (2) sitting on boards or committees. For the asset-based model to work, leadership must also mean taking on a role in building and leading micro-communities, mentoring less-experienced community members, and creating powerful Jewish experiences that take place in these smaller clusters. Essentially, this means a shift from a lead-ership model focused on advancing institutions to a leadership model focused on advancing Jewish life and community building.

What This Looks Like in Real Life

Making such a substantial change in the way we run our organizations spawns fear and anxiety, but it truly works when given time and commit-ment. Here I would like to provide several examples of how asset-based community development can actually function. Below is a story about the successful integration of community partnerships:

Consider a local art school with a large number of Jewish students who are currently under-engaged by the existing Jewish community. When the community leaders connect with the school, they discover that the school is in need of places to showcase art produced by the students. Through some simple mapping work, the two organizations envision the idea of an art exhibition of student work first at a local synagogue and then in a central public space in the city. But rather than moving forward immediately and planning this event, they first take time to engage others. The art school reaches out to dozens of artists who are seeking a place to display their work, and the synagogue connects with under-engaged congregants who are art lovers. Through careful work and by utilizing community partners, something really special happens that goes beyond simply hosting a successful program. Both organizations succeed in reaching new and diverse types of people, and in the process they help rebrand themselves as more open, innovative, and attractive to the larger community.

In this example, everyone wins, and both organizations benefit.

Next, consider another example from Penn Hillel, in which JRP student interns were asked to become creators of Jewish life for their friends and even to lead text-based discussions. In the early days, many people questioned the wisdom of this approach. Did student interns have the knowledge and the confidence to create an authentic Shabbat dinner experience? Could they facilitate a text-based Jewish conversation? Or did they need a professional educator to lead these experiences? The following story highlights the surprising results of our experiments:

A JRP student intern named Molly was struggling to figure out what conversation she should have at the Shabbat dinner she was hosting in her sorority house. We played with a number of different topics and a variety of different textual sources, but in the end she was still hesitant. Finally, she said that while she liked all of these formal topics and the sources I offered, in order to really host the meal, she would need to do it in a way that was

authentic to her and to her friends. She said that I would just
have to trust her.

In the end, Molly hosted a Shabbat dinner that lasted more
than four hours for nearly twenty of her friends who never went
to Hillel and who had never had a Shabbat meal together. At a
certain point in the meal, Molly asked an open-ended question
about what being Jewish meant to each of them. Her friends
jumped in, sharing their own Jewish stories and positive memories, as well as expressions of insecurity and guilt about their level
of Jewish involvement. In the months and years that followed,
nearly all of those students found their way into deep learning initiatives run by JRP and became creators of Jewish life for
others.[19]

While it is clear that the experience those students had at Shabbat dinner
was qualitatively different from the kind of text study one of Penn Hillel's educators could have created and facilitated, something else amazing happened. A community of friends who lived, studied, and socialized
together became a Jewish community for the first time. For most of these
students, it was the first serious conversation they had had about Judaism
in their lives and certainly the most serious one outside the confines of
a Jewish institutional space. We created a context in which the students
could create their own Jewish experience in a way that encouraged them to
relate to one another. This experience would not have been possible had
those same students been encouraged to attend a Shabbat dinner at Hillel
or even if Hillel had sent a charismatic Hillel rabbi to the sorority house
to lead the conversation. In either of these situations, the students would
have been forced into the "passive client" relationship, and the experience
would have been shaped more by the relationship with Hillel or with the
rabbi than with each other.

Changing Our Thinking Changes Our Reality

I once heard an executive coach say that "as leaders, we are responsible
for what we think." As leaders, the way we think about our work and
how we approach the challenges facing our organizations have dramatic
implications on our decision making. When we focus on our problems

and how to fix them, we create vast unintended consequences ranging from disempowering community members to undermining the social connections that hold communities together. But when we work within the framework of asset-based community building, a whole new set of possibilities emerges. We can transform people's lives rather than keeping our institutions afloat. We can get resources to the people who need them and unlock the hidden potential of these social networks to be creators of Jewish life. When we start the conversation about the Jewish future with what's right, we go beyond optimism and positivity to create a paradigm shift that can free us from all of the pitfalls of being stuck in our own sense of crisis and decline.

Of course, leadership should never run away from problems. Good leaders spend a great deal of time and every available tool trying to understand the complexity of problems facing their communities. The key is to spend at least as much time and energy focusing on building on what is right as we do trying to fix what is wrong. Only when this balance is achieved can we truly gain the kind of knowledge and perspective that is necessary to approach those challenges in an effective, meaningful, and transformative way.

Questions for Further Consideration

1. In reflecting on your own leadership and the focus of your organization, what are the problems and challenges that form your deficiency map?

2. In what ways does your organization fit into a deficiency-based approach? In what ways might you inadvertently trap power, expertise, and resources in the hands of a few?

3. Do the communities you work with sometimes end up fitting into the passive client role discussed above? If so, when and how?

4. Try to draw an asset map for your organization and your community. Start by thinking about the different types of social capital that exist: who are the connectors, the mavens, and the salesmen in your communities? How are you and your organization

connected to these people? If you are not, how can you begin to build those connections?

5. What about geographic capital? Can you discover where people live, work, and gather? When you do, can you then find out where Jewish life thrives and where it struggles? What are some ways to empower people to create Jewish life in the places where it struggles?

6. What about community partners? Are there ways that your organization can cooperate with others in the area to work smarter, cheaper, and faster to reach even more people?

7. How much of your work takes place in a formal Jewish building? What would it look like to add Jewish opportunities that could take place outside of the building?

8. When you think about the events sponsored by your organization, how many of them are designed for macro-communities versus micro-communities? What would it look like to add more options for people to be part of Jewish micro-communities?

9. What would it look like if your organization moved toward a model that favored empowerment rather than service?

9

Peer-to-Peer Engagement

Throughout the previous chapters, there have been many references to "peer-to-peer engagement." Here we will explore the depth of the art and science of peer-to-peer engagement in order to maximize the impact that this kind of relationship building and community organizing can have on your organization. A peer-to-peer engagement model is much more than simply having leaders reach out to their peers to try to plan programs or to more effectively recruit for existing programmatic offers. Rather, it is a methodology that focuses on building deep relationships and on activating the latent energy and passion of hundreds and even thousands of Jews who are under-engaged.[1] In this way, peer-to-peer engagement can have a dramatic and transformative impact on how an organization operates and how it makes a difference in the lives of the communities with whom it works.

How Peer-to-Peer Engagement Works at Penn Hillel

In a normal year, JRP at Penn Hillel recruits an average of 160 peer engagement student interns. Most of them are recruited when a staff person or another student intern builds a relationship with them and helps connect them to one of the various JRP initiatives, which are carefully designed based on the students' interests, social network, and class year. Potential student interns are attracted to the initiative because of JRP's great reputation, the students' desire to grow in their Judaism, and the strength of their relationships with the recruiter. JRP focuses its recruitment on students who are not yet engaged in Jewish life on campus but who are leaders and connectors among social networks with large concentrations of disconnected Jewish students.

The student interns begin their fellowship with a two-day immersive retreat focused on training for engagement and community building among the cohort. Once back on campus, the different intern groups meet once a week throughout the year, focusing primarily on the kind of Jewish learning that matches the educational philosophy described in chapter 7. Leadership development and training are also woven into these weekly meetings.

Each student intern is asked to take the Jewish inspiration and confidence they find in the weekly meetings and use it to create relationships with sixty additional students from similar Jewish backgrounds. They work within that network of relationships to build initiatives that have the capacity to engage hundreds more students without ever having to leave their social group, go to another building, join some Jewish club, or pay dues. These initiatives normally generate two or three events each semester.

In a typical year, this cohort of student interns engages approximately thirteen hundred students. It is easy to see in our tracking data that there are hundreds of students each year who, were it not for these initiatives, would not be engaged in any kind of Jewish life. Because of JRP, they end up having Shabbat dinners, Jewish conversations, or holiday celebrations with their friends on a monthly basis.

Community Organizing and Peer-to-Peer Engagement

Often the leadership of organizations is so focused on short-term goals that they overlook the most important preliminary steps required to inspire a community to action. Before leaders can begin the work of building new initiatives or advancing a community organization, serious time must be devoted to building relationships, uncovering feelings, and telling personal stories.[2]

Why are these feelings and stories so important to being a successful engagement organization? Personal storytelling is the key to accessing the deepest experiences, expectations, and values at play in someone's life. It helps the teller to become more aware of her own Jewish story with all of its ups and downs,[3] and it prompts you, the listener, to think about how the story resonates with you emotionally or intellectually. Storytelling does more than create a space for this kind of personal reflection; it is also one of the most profound ways to build intimate relationships. But even more than that, once we feel connected to another person, other things emerge out of our shared stories. For example, as people begin to talk about what's most important to them, they often also end up sharing the ways in which they are unsatisfied with the status quo. Rather than getting stuck on everything that's wrong, the best engagers can use the sense of shared dissatisfaction to provoke a kind of creative tension between the way the world is and the way it ought to be.[4] This tension and the desire to resolve it become the starting point and the catalyst for purposeful action.[5]

> "You need to be smart to know how to tell a story properly. But you need to be even smarter to know how to listen to a story properly."
> —Rabbi Shalom Dov Ber of Lubavitch

Three Steps to Organizing: The Story of Self, the Story of Us, the Story of Now

Community organizers use a simple three-step process developed by Marshall Ganz at Kennedy School of Government at Harvard University to use storytelling to provoke positive action. This model creates a wonderful template that we can apply to the work of Jewish engagement.

1. **The story of self** communicates who you are and how you came to be. By telling this story, you also express the values that are calling you to act.

2. **The story of us** communicates the connections we have to something larger than ourselves. This includes the Jewish people, the power of smaller communities, and shared values. Rather than speaking about what "I" am called to do, the story of us is collective.

> "If I am not for myself, who will be for me? If I am only for myself, what am I? If not now, when?"
> —Rabbi Hillel

3. **The story of now** communicates an urgent challenge to those values that demands immediate action. Ganz explains, "In a story of now, story and strategy overlap because a key element of hope is a strategy—a credible vision of how to get from here to there."[6]

In practical terms, these three steps provide guidelines for the kinds of conversations that a leader can have as he is building relationships. Whether this takes place one-on-one over coffee or in small groups, the process is the same. Start by devoting serious time to hearing the story of the person you're trying to engage and sharing your own. Find the different points of commonality among the various stories, and then look for the ways those collective stories create some imperative to action.

Here is one example of how this played out at Hillel:

Lyla was a sophomore student intern for the Jewish Renaissance Project. While she loved the weekly learning, she was totally stuck when it came to planning external events. She sat down with the rabbi who was advising the group, and she said, "I don't know what kind of event to host. I want to do a good job and fulfill my obligation, but I really don't care one way or the other. Can you just tell me what I should do?" The rabbi paused before responding, and rather than answering her question, he got her thinking about her own Jewish story. Eventually she admitted that although she didn't like High Holy Day services, she went as a child to please her parents and grandparents. She was turned off by a service that seemed to present God in a way she couldn't understand, in a language she didn't speak. She wanted to be a "good Jew" but felt like the things she was supposed to do didn't quite fit.

The rabbi then shared his story. He often felt the same way growing up and when he was in college. She asked him, "What changed then? How did you end up being a rabbi?" He talked about a few of the teachers and role models who helped him to understand what the prayers meant beyond the literal meaning of the words. He shared a few examples that seemed to resonate with her. Then the rabbi asked her, "Do you think there are others in your sorority who feel the same way?" She said, "Of course. We all went to services together and all felt guilty afterward because we didn't feel anything." The rabbi said, "Lyla, I think we've found your initiative. Let's get all of your friends who feel really Jewish but don't like services together so that we can talk about it, learn more about it, and hopefully get to a place where you can all start feeling better about it." She loved that idea and gathered ten of her friends to meet with the rabbi every other week for the rest of the semester to talk about what services could mean even for someone who didn't believe in the literal meaning of the prayers.

In Lyla's case, the act of storytelling transformed a moment that was focused on what program to do into a moment focused on how to make a difference in the lives of her friends. Rather than letting the focus be on executing a successful event, the rabbi got her to tell her story. He then shared the parts of his story that helped create common ground. Then there was a moment when Lyla could see that she needed to do something about her dissatisfaction with services. What happened next wasn't a program; it was a set of Jewish experiences that grew out of Lyla's own personal Jewish story. She also helped her friends tell their Jewish stories and then invited them to become co-creators in shaping their experiences, rather than just consumers. Had Hillel just offered a class about finding meaning in the High Holy Day liturgy without all that storytelling, Lyla and her friends would never have been engaged, because they don't go to Hillel and they never read the listserv that promotes Hillel events. The ten students who *would* have taken that class would have been regulars who already felt comfortable in Hillel. This example highlights just how different the outcome can be when we start with stories rather than logistics.

This same methodology can be deployed in synagogues, Federations, and JCCs with similar success regardless of audience. The key is to have intentional personal conversations with a large number of people who are not already in formal leadership roles and to figure out how to channel all of this Jewish energy in constructive ways that benefit both the individuals involved as well as their larger social networks.

Axioms for Organizers by Fred Ross Sr. (1989)
Compiled by Rabbi Noah Farkas

- **The power of organizing:** Organizing is providing people with the opportunity to become aware of their own capabilities and potential.

- **Duty of organizer:** The duty of the organizer is to provide people with the opportunity to work for what they believe in.
- **Doing it "for" people:** If you think you can do it for people, you've stopped understanding what it means to be an organizer.
- **Lead by pushing:** An organizer is a leader who does not lead but gets behind the people and pushes.
- **Leadership:** You don't develop new leaders; you push people into taking action by refusing to do it yourself. You are then providing them the opportunity to become aware of their own capabilities.
- **"From the heart":** How can you move others unless you are moved yourself?
- **Follow-up:** Ninety percent of organizing is follow-up.
- **Questions**: When you are tempted to make a statement, ask a question.

The Art and Impact of a Great Coffee Date

The art of Jewish storytelling provides a great rhetorical framework for how to generate a new set of Jewish experiences for people in your communities. One of the most effective tools for unlocking the power of a personal story is through the art of the coffee date.

Sitting and talking about the important things in life over a cup of coffee has always been an important part of college. While adults may not always find the time to sit in a coffee shop discussing the meaning of life, we too have the desire to get away from all the tumult of our homes and offices and sit with another person in order to build a deeper personal relationship, and to reflect on the most important issues in our lives. Of course, the same interaction can happen over drinks, lunch, or even a walk in the park. For the sake of simplicity, however, I use the term "coffee date" in this chapter to refer to any kind of one-on-one relationship-building conversation.

Over the past ten years, Hillels all over North America have taken the casual coffee date and developed it into a transformative methodology for engaging a wide variety of Jews who are not already reached by the offerings of Hillel's core programs. The term "coffee date" is deceptive in its simplicity. How, you may wonder, can having coffee with someone translate into renewed Jewish engagement or organizational transformation? The answer is, it can't. Simply sitting down to get to know someone over coffee is not enough. For the coffee date to really live up to its full potential, it must be executed the right way. Therefore, let me showcase a workable template for the ideal coffee date.

Taking Coffee Dates to the Next Level

While great Hillel professionals and educators have always used the coffee date to build relationships with new students, the entire Hillel system took this to a new level beginning a decade ago with the launch of Hillel International's new strategic plan. In past iterations, Hillel's mission had focused more on programmatic participation, but the new plan was different in that it was focused on the impact that Hillel could have on students regardless of whether they ever came to a Hillel event. In this way, "relationship-based engagement" became the centerpiece of Hillel's work. This new focus on relationships was greatly amplified throughout the Hillel system when the Jim Joseph Foundation made a generous grant to Hillel International to develop an engagement model that paired a Senior Jewish Educator (SJE) with a cohort of peer-to-peer student interns who were part of a new project called the Campus Entrepreneurs Initiative (CEI).[7] Over the next five years, the art of the coffee date was perfected and the data confirmed in hard numbers what we already assumed to be true about the power of relationships.

Here are just a few highlights from the data that was collected during the first two years of the project:

- In the first year of CEI/SJE, the initiative reached a total of 13,883 students on seventeen different campuses, 60 percent of whom had little or no prior contact with Hillel.[8]
- When SJEs included "Jewish talk" as part of the coffee date, students had much greater levels of Jewish growth.[9]
- When SJEs spoke only about other matters (e.g., school, relationships, sports), there was no measurable increase in Jewish activity from one year to the next.[10]

- The more time a person spent talking Jewishly with an SJE, the greater the impact. The greatest impact seems to have occurred with students who met with a SJE six or more times throughout a year.[11]

Coffee Dating as an Engagement Strategy

When an organization moves from a purely program-based model to a hybrid model that includes peer-to-peer engagement, the definition of what it means to be a leader also changes. In the classic Program Model, leadership is about sitting on committees, making important decisions, publicizing programs, and recruiting attendees. In the peer-to-peer model, leadership also includes building relationships with the populations of people an organization is trying to engage. Rather than making decisions and figuring out what works for the community at large, this model of leadership is about getting to know people so that they become co-creators and partners in developing their community.[12]

One of the best ways to accomplish this goal is through the simple act of a coffee date. Reaching out to someone new in a personal way changes the whole dynamic. No longer are leaders trying to recruit new people to a program; they are asking to get to know them. Rather than asking the new people to come to them, the leaders are instead going to meet them on neutral ground. Another important difference between program planning and coffee dating is that it gives leaders the power to make intentional choices about who to reach out to and when. A coffee date breaks down many of the social, geographic, and cultural barriers that often separate those who show up at programs and those who don't by bringing the relationship to the Engagement Jews wherever they may be.

Although it may appear casual and informal, there is an art to making the most of the coffee date as an engagement strategy. A wise and simple format for a coffee date was developed by Rabbi Joel Nickerson when he was the Senior Jewish Educator for the Jewish Renaissance Project at Penn Hillel. The goal in meeting students, he said, was "to open up a closed book, to begin flipping through the pages, and to think about how a new page can be written."[13]

A coffee date has to be two things at once. First, it needs to be approached in an open way that has no agenda. A leader cannot enter a coffee date with specific, institutional-based engagement goals in mind (like getting someone to join, get involved, or donate). Second, the coffee date has to have a greater purpose than relationship building. The goal is to help Engagement Jews find the next set of opportunities for Jewish growth and to help them write the next page of their Jewish journey.

Coffee dates have the power to break down boundaries and assumptions people have about the Jewish community and its leaders. For so many students, Judaism is for the synagogue or a rabbi's office. It connotes proper etiquette and represents distance between their personal reality and what is considered the Jewish ideal.[14] By contrast, a coffee date is simple and more accessible. It happens on the students' own terms, on familiar territory.

Once arranged, the conversation that takes place at these coffee dates is both organic and intentional. We have defined the ideal coffee date as including the following four components, either all in the initial meeting or in several subsequent meetings:[15]

1. **Investigation:** Getting someone to tell his story, including the telling of his Jewish story—with all the positive and negative twists and turns.[16] While it's nice to be able to tell a rabbi what inspires you about Judaism, the real goal is to get folks to share their Jewish baggage.

2. **Validation:** Helping someone come to understand that she is not alone in her feelings and experiences. Sometimes leaders accomplish this by sharing parts of their own Jewish story. Other times, what a person really needs is help placing her experiences in a larger context. The key is to assure her that she is not alone.

3. **Provocation:** Once a strong rapport has been established, it's the job of the leader to provoke the person being engaged, challenging him to see beyond himself to some alternative possibilities for his own Jewish life or the life of the community. This is probably the hardest part of the coffee date, but as the research suggests, this is the most important. This is when people truly grow and step forward into the next step on their Jewish journey.

4. **Invitation:** The final aspect of the ideal coffee date is an invitation to take a next step, regardless of what that step might be.

A master leader in the field of engagement, Hart Levine began his career as a student leader at Penn Hillel. Hart founded an initiative called Heart to Heart, whose goal was not only to support the existing programs and communities on campus, but also to find ways to reach out to other students and to connect them to new opportunities to explore Judaism.[17] Hart had a gift for inviting someone to study Torah with him or to join him for a Shabbat dinner, but more importantly Hart was able to inspire others to do the same, so that he recruited a small army of students who wanted to make leadership more about helping Jews find their way than about getting Jews to show up at a program.

For Hart, leadership was about one-on-one or small-group engagement that was laser focused on making an impact on people's Jewish identities. He was not trying to influence people to practice his brand of Judaism; rather, he simply wanted to invite them to be part of something he loved in a personal and authentic way. His goal was never quantity, but always quality. In the end, Hart and the people he inspired managed to reach hundreds of students on Penn's campus in ways that were extraordinarily warm, welcoming, and impactful. Whether it was a Shabbat dinner, a chance to do Jewish learning, or simply a one-on-one Jewish mentoring session, the students that Heart to Heart reached over the years each grew in significant ways.

Imagine what American Judaism might look like if Hart's model of leadership were expanded. Most successful boards expect their members to attend meetings, make donations or spearhead fundraising, and do committee work. Think of the how the impact of these leadership roles would be dramatically expanded if peer-to-peer engagement were added to the requirements. What if every board member were charged with building relationships with thirty Jews who are not already connected to Jewish life? Or hosting monthly Shabbat dinners for people who are not affiliated with Jewish organizations? Or starting a

> "If you want to pull someone out of the mire, it is not enough to stand above him with an outstretched hand. You yourself have to climb into the muck, immersing yourself fully in the mud. Only then can you grasp him with both hands and pull him out with you."
>
> —Rabbi Shlomo of Karlin

study group or Jewish book club for people who are not otherwise engaged in Jewish learning? Other goals might include creating a giving circle for Jewish causes for those who are not yet participating in Jewish philanthropy, or mentoring a young family who is struggling to juggle parenting small children and building a Jewish life, or helping someone learn a new Jewish skill like actively participating in the services or how to read Torah.[18]

The creative possibilities for how an organization can redefine what leadership means are endless. And so are the rewards.

Rather than modeling how to serve institutions, this new kind of leadership is about reinvigorating Judaism and building stronger communities. Fascinating research has been done in the inner city that suggests that personal mentoring has more power to change the life of an at-risk youth than any other intervention.[19] If we want to do more than sustain the community and the institutions we have, we need some tools for transformation. The tool of mentoring is one such asset at our disposal. By transforming the job description of a leader to include mentoring in addition to the classic roles of decision maker, donor, and program planner, Jewish organizations could dramatically expand their capacity to make a deep and lasting impact in the Jewish lives of so many more people each year. And it can all start with a simple cup of coffee.

How Coffee Dates Work in Congregations

Rabbi Joel Nickerson

As soon as I started my job as a rabbi at a congregation in Los Angeles, I began implementing the tools and strategies developed during my time as the Senior Jewish Educator at Penn Hillel. I was hoping to replicate the results of the engagement work already proving to be successful on college campuses around the country. For the past five years, I have spent significant time trying to understand how synagogues can utilize the strategies that have already transformed the landscape of Jewish engagement on college campuses. From the hundreds of one-on-one coffee dates and other engagement work I have done at my synagogue over the years, I have come to understand that we are at a key turning point in the development of synagogue life. Without a greater shift toward this type of relational work, we will be doing a great disservice to our congregants, and we may end up jeopardizing the entire synagogue model. It is unbelievable, and frankly disturbing, how many members of my community have sat down with me for coffee and told me that it was the first time they had sat down with a clergyperson for a one-on-one conversation since they went through the *b'nei mitzvah* process at the age of thirteen. And these are people in their thirties, forties, fifties, and sixties! That means there are a significant number of Jewish adults out there who have gone twenty to forty years without a substantial Jewish conversation with someone who is trained as a Jewish educator and spiritual advisor.

The conversations I have during these coffee dates, meals, and sometimes over a beer at a local bar are almost identical in their format to the conversations I had with college students at Penn. And when you strip away the layers of complexity that come with adulthood, the foundational questions are almost identical:

- How do I have meaningful and fulfilling relationships with my loved ones?
- What does success look like at work?
- Why am I doing what I'm doing?
- How do I find balance and search for a greater purpose in my life?
- What, if anything, does Judaism have to offer me in my everyday life?
- What is my legacy?

You can't answer these questions by bringing a guest speaker to the synagogue, offering a multi-part learning series, or talking about these themes at Shabbat services. The best way to address these existential questions is through one-on-one relationship building and engagement.

Whether you are a member of the clergy, a Jewish professional working at a synagogue, or a lay leader, here are a few ways you can get started:

1. **Take the conversations off-site:** I have found that the best conversations take place outside the walls of the synagogue and outside the confines of a formal Jewish program (you cannot have one of these conversations at the Shabbat *Oneg*).

2. **Track your relationships:** The success of relationship-based engagement is linked to your willingness and ability to track the relationships you make. It's the only way to really know what you're doing and to help you remember how to follow up. The RMS20 (Relational Managing System) app and a web-based service called Hineynu21 are two tools among many that are out there today.

3. **Connect on social media:** It's time to begin building relationships with your constituency by connecting with them on social media. They should know what's going on in your life, and you should be able to participate in conversations with them through social media outlets, such as Facebook, Twitter, Instagram, and others.

Is Peer-to-Peer Engagement Just Proselytizing?

When I am presenting these ideas to groups, this is the point at which people seem to cross their arms or withdraw a bit. It can be uncomfortable to think about reaching out and bringing Judaism to our friends. We worry about how much time or energy it would take to add these responsibilities to our already busy lives. We feel awkward about asking our friends to reflect on their relationship with Judaism. For many liberal Jews, religion is personal, and this kind of engagement may seem like proselytizing or an evangelical crusade.

I totally understand that feeling. This work is hard, and it may feel uncomfortable at first. And yet it is so important that we do it anyway. Given the changing nature of Jewish community in America, a "business as usual" approach will not foster the kind of change that we all want and need. Given the situation and the challenges we face, working harder, working smarter, and going outside our comfort zone is exactly what we need to do.

Peer-to-peer methodology is decidedly *not* proselytizing. We are not being manipulative or intrusive. We do not assume that we have the truth and need to convince others. Rather, peer-to-peer methodology is about meeting people where they are. We are not there to fix people or save them, just to help them take the next step in their Jewish journey. And this, by the way, is what most people want. Studies show that Jewish Americans are interested in getting more connected but they don't know how, in part because they perceive Jewish organizations as insular and unwelcoming.[22] The final reason that peer-to-peer engagement is different than proselytizing is that the goal is not for people to become just like you, but for them to be able to grow into the kind of Jew that they want to be. Focusing on their unique Jewish growth without any other agenda ensures that the relationship building is genuine and not mixed with a conflicting set of ulterior motives.

Shifting from Programs to a Curriculum of Experiences

Once we begin to make peer-to-peer engagement part of our standard operating procedures, we need to create a real and intentional plan for how to move people from one experience to the next. This involves not just changing the leadership models of our organizations but shifting the very essence of our organizations from an emphasis on individual programs to an emphasis on a curated set of ongoing Jewish experiences.

One of the biggest challenges we face is limited bandwidth. There never seems to be enough time or staff to do everything that needs to be done in the short term, let alone the energy or time to do the hard work of longer-term planning. And yet, good leadership knows that this kind of longer-term work is essential to the future success of an organization. For these reasons, it has become a common best practice to invest resources in strategic plans or capital campaigns, even hiring outside consultants to help. Most of this work, though, is focused on the needs and health of the institution. It is rare that organizations invest the same kind of time and money to develop strategies for how to impact people's lives. Clearly, the best strategic plan that ensures institutional health matters only if it can create the relationships, opportunities, and communities that inspire more vibrant expressions of Jewish life.

One simple model for how to do strategic planning around engagement goals looks something like figure 11—we call it the "swirl of engagement."[23] The swirl represents the process of developing a relationship with an individual or an engagement plan with a particular target population. The dots along the swirl represent sequential steps and progress in that person's level of engagement. The first dot might be an introductory email, the second a coffee date, the third an invitation for Shabbat dinner, and so on.

The way to apply the swirl of engagement is to start with the mission of your organization and stay focused on what impact you want to have on a particular individual or community in several years.[24] Once leadership has developed a larger vision for the future, the next step is to recruit a group of engagers, decide what kinds of "touches" (like phone calls, coffee dates, and programmatic participation) would work best for your situation, and then make some specific decisions about how to execute the plan. This includes decisions like making a clear timeline and assigning different engagers to different populations so everyone knows what they have to do and by when. The engagement plans need to be carefully calibrated so that the process feels seamless, simple, and authentic for the populations you

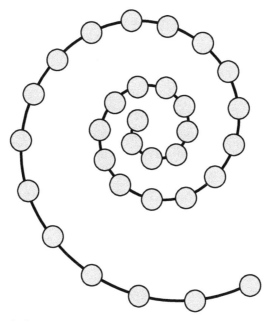

Figure 11. The swirl of engagement

are trying to engage and concrete enough to be easily accomplished by the people doing the engagement.

As the Yiddish proverb reminds us, "People plan and God laughs." It is important that any engagement plan remain flexible. While relationships are the natural resource that fuels this system and while planning and intentionality are essential, they should not lead to mechanical or impersonal relationships. The essence of the swirl is to ensure that organizations are committed to really engage people in a deep and ongoing way and that they avoid the traps of one-off events. Therefore, while the starting point on the swirl might be relatively uniform for each of the individuals or communities you are trying to reach, where it goes from there really depends on how the relationships develop.

For Federations, the swirl model can be used to engage more volunteer leaders and more donors. For Hillels, it can be used to reach more students. For day schools, it can be used to network and recruit a larger number of students or to deepen the educational impact of the school on the families of current students. In general, I recommend developing a different swirl of engagement for each population. These different groups could be divided by interest, social network, or stage of life.

Following are several specific groupings and ideas about what the swirl of engagement might look like for them.

Group #1: The Regulars

Organizations often forget to be intentional about how to enrich the Jewish lives of the "regulars"[25] because they are already highly engaged. I see this play out in Hillel all the time. While the Engagement Jews are participating in deep Jewish learning and thinking, Empowerment Jews sometimes end up spending all of their time in meetings discussing logistics and budgets, without making room for the deeper Jewish questions. To really build an impact organization, there needs to be a plan for meaningful engagement even for the regulars who may not at first glance seem to need or want it.

For this group, the goal of the swirl of engagement is to add a new layer to their Jewish experiences that goes beyond attendance and/or leadership. Again, the key here is that these are not programs offered by a committee or advertised to the whole community, but opportunities geared specifically for the regulars, such as small, intimate gatherings where they can meet new people, engage in inspirational Jewish learning, or learn new Jewish skills—anything that is highly impactful and not focused on the business of running the organization.

Group #2: The Occasionals

The "occasionals" are the Jews who continue to pay dues or make an annual gift but attend events only a few times a year. The best example of this group is the family who belongs to a synagogue but comes to services only on the High Holy Days or for the bar or bat mitzvah ceremony of friends. This group is low-hanging fruit if they are engaged the right way. Jews in this category tend to be Jewishly self-directed enough that they are willing to affiliate but not enough to be interested in attending the current programmatic or religious offerings. It has been my experience that a significant reason that this group of Jews fails to show up is that they find many organizations socially and religiously inaccessible, intimidating, or irrelevant. Therefore, even though they are technically affiliated, they can still be considered Engagement Jews.

For this group, typical programming, even when it's repackaged, will not be successful. Rather, they will require a personal relationship and customized Jewish experiences. I would suggest in-home hospitality for Shabbat dinners several times a year, coffee dates with leadership, invitations to learning groups with others who share similar interests, and opportunities for them to act as peer-engagers for those less plugged into the organization.

Group #3: The Non-Members

People who live near your organization but who are not members are often given last priority and the least attention. And yet if we really want to usher in a renaissance in American Judaism, we all have to do more to reach out to every single Jew. These Jews will need special and personal invitations to be part of small, customized Jewish experiences. They will most likely not respond to any kind of formal marketing or programming, but rather will need a personal relationship in order to be engaged.

Non-members will respond to coffee dates focused on mapping out potentially interesting new Jewish experiences for them, invitations to Shabbat dinners from familiar faces, and receiving different Jewish care packages throughout the year such as fresh-baked challah on Fridays or *mishloach manot* baskets at Purim. These touches will help make them feel cared about by the organization and more connected to other Jewish people regardless of their membership status.

A Peer-to-Peer Model for Engaging a Higher Percentage of "At Risk" (of Disaffiliation) Households with Teens

Rabbi Alan Silverstein

Our community of over nine hundred households has invested time and energy thinking about how to stem the tide of families that disaffiliate in the post–bar/bat mitzvah years. Our concern is not just about losing members. We know that the teenage years are critical for Jewish identity formation that affects the future Jewish lives of both the teens and their families. Even though our synagogue was seen as a success because our participation numbers for programs like USY and Shabbat Teen Schmooze and Minyan were much higher than at other synagogues, we were still serving only one-third of eligible adolescents and their households.

When we looked deeper into the data, we found that the two-thirds, the unengaged teens, had other friends who were also under-engaged. We realized that these networks were a great untapped resource that could help us dramatically increase the number of teens that we reach. As a remedy, we employed peer-to-peer focus groups and coffee dates with families and teens who had social capital, leading to the following action plan.

First, we determined that we would maintain and strengthen existing teen offerings such as Kadimah/USY, day school, Jewish summer camp, and Shabbat Teen Schmooze and Minyan. Second, in response to focus groups and coffee dates, we created a new, specially designed in-synagogue Hebrew high school for new people not already connected, and we held it on the same evening as USY/Kadimah, to encourage cross-participation. The resulting "Teen Night" increased overall teen participation in weekly activities by 33 percent.

Focus groups and coffee dates also gave us valuable information about how social action projects could be used to reach even more under-engaged teens, their families, and their social networks. Again and again we heard about the impact of our *b'nei mitzvah* "mitzvah projects." Building on that success, we developed an array of new service options that reached nearly one hundred other teens who were not already active in Jewish service.

The same thing happened with our Jewish cultural options for teens. The work we did with focus groups and coffee dates led to creation of new portals to entry points into Jewish life for dozens of additional teens.

In the end, through our engagement of "connectors" and social networks among underserved households of teens, we now have doubled the percentage of teens (from 33 percent to 66 percent) connected to some kind of formal Jewish group activity. Additionally, many teens now have multiple connecting points. We learned that neither adolescents nor their families can be forced into one cookie-cutter approach. One size does not fit all. The key for this transformation was to make sure that both teens and parents were part of the discussion and partners in the creation of new Jewish opportunities. We could no longer rely simply on staff-planned programming. By doing the engagement work first, before we planned programs, and by increasing the community's ownership in what Jewish life looked like, we have reached dramatically larger numbers of teens and in doing so have strengthened their entire family's connection to Judaism.

Empowerment Through Distributed Leadership

How do organizations that are already strapped for resources and time successfully engage post-institutional Jews who seem to demand endless levels of customization and personalization in their Jewish experiences? One of the answers to that question is for Jewish organizations to adopt a model of distributed leadership that empowers people to be creators of Jewish experiences for themselves and their social networks.

Peer-to-peer engagement is the delivery system for how this empowerment takes place. No matter how many staff and professionals an organization has, they will never be able to be all things to all people all the time. Peer-to-peer engagement is a great way to dramatically increase the number and diversity of people who feel ownership for and access to Jewish life. Because peer engagers are not professionals or experts inside an institution, they can reach people where they are and build bridges with networks of people that professionals have never been able to reach.

Peer-to-peer engagement also changes and even deepens what leadership means. It's not just about sitting on boards and helping to plan new programs, but about building relationships, getting people to tell their Jewish stories, and asking them to be partners in the next set of steps in their Jewish journey. When the peer-to-peer model is used to complement a strong and successful model run by professionals, a whole new world of Jewish possibilities is opened, and Jewish organizations reach more people in more ways than they ever could before.

Questions for Further Consideration

1. Imagine you are asked to tell your own Jewish story. What are some of the key experiences, people, and ideas that have made you the Jew you are today? Please include both positive and negative examples—both are essential parts of your story.

2. When you think about your own Jewish story, where do you see a gap between your Jewish life as it is and your Jewish life as you would want it to be? What actions would you need to take to help close that gap?

3. If you map out the people you know, whether they are connected to your organization or not, who are the ideal people to tap to become peer engagers? Who are the people who have the passion and the social capital to be able to reach out to

networks of Jews who are not currently engaged by your organization?

4. How would you talk to or train peer engagers to help them get over the fear of starting Jewish conversations with the people they know?

5. What are the different types of populations that your organization could engage? What would the "swirl of engagement" look like for each of these groups?

6. What kind of additional resources (professional, volunteer, or financial) would your organization need to create a number of swirls of engagement and build an intentional plan for further Jewish growth for each of these populations?

Conclusion

Not long after the Children of Israel leave Egypt, Moses disappears into the cloud on Mount Sinai for forty days and forty nights. You can imagine how terrifying it must have been for the people, not knowing if their leader would ever return. In that moment of uncertainty, the Children of Israel, desperate for a sense of security and of connection to God, create the Golden Calf. The Torah makes this explicit when it says, "Come, make us a god who will go before us, for that man Moses, who brought us up out of the land of Egypt—we do not know what has happened to him" (Exodus 32:1). If they couldn't have the real connection to God through Moses, they were willing to build a stand-in—a material object that could replace Moses and the God he represented. It is through fear and panic that the Children of Israel commit what is considered to be their greatest failure of faith.

Just a few chapters earlier, the Children of Israel were commanded to create the *Mishkan*, a portable sanctuary that they could take with them while they travel through the desert.[1] At its very core, the *Mishkan* was more than just a space to perform the various sacrificial rituals required. It was a material object designed to help the Children of Israel feel close to God. When we put the *Mishkan* and the Golden Calf side by side, it is hard to understand why one was sanctioned while the other was a great sin. Both were material objects. Both were infused with a sense of holiness. Both were intended to help the people connect with God.

What separates these two objects, making one a holy religious tool and the other an idol?

The medieval Jewish commentator Rashi rereads God's commandment to build a tabernacle in the following way: "Let them make me a house for holiness" (Rashi on Exodus 25:8). Rashi shifts the focus from the object to the space. The object is just a material structure, but the space creates the potential for holiness.[2] In other words, the *Mishkan* was holy not because of what it was, but because of what it could do. This then explains the real difference between it and the Golden Calf. The Golden Calf was not intended to bring people closer to God; it was intended to *be* a god. It was not intended to be a tool to help people worship; it was intended to be worshiped itself. This story clarifies the distinction between a holy object and an idol, but in real life, the power of idolatry is more subtle and more seductive. In today's world, idolatry seems like an archaic concept. It's easy to refrain from pretending that statues are gods. But even now, idolatry occurs when we infuse things with more meaning than they really deserve.[3] Money, technology, success, and youth are tools that can help us focus on what really matters, but more often than not they are glorified as the goals of our lives.

"Religion has often suffered from the tendency to become an end unto itself ... to become self-seeking.... Yet the task of religion is to challenge the stabilization of values. Religion is not for religion's sake but for God's sake."

—Abraham Joshua Heschel

Leadership in the contemporary American Jewish experience can also be fraught with a kind of organizational idolatry. This happens when we think of an organization as an end unto itself rather than a simply a tool intended to fulfill a particular mission at a particular time. While it may not be the kind of grave sin depicted in the Torah, the problem with this kind of organizational idolatry is that it values past success and future survival over all other values and in doing so stunts an organization's ability to keep evolving and renewing itself for each consecutive generation of Jews.

We all know that the road ahead for Jewish institutions will be a difficult one. As America and American Jews change, will synagogues, Federations, JCCs, and denominations be able to survive? I suggest that our survival depends on whether we treat these organizations like the Golden Calf or like the *Mishkan*: Is continued survival an end unto itself? Or do we treat our organizations like the *Mishkan*, important and even holy, but focused on something larger than itself? Can we find a way to manage our own fears about the future of our organizations so that we can recapture the deeper and more inspirational reason for their existence, to help inspire and empower Jewish people to live the most vibrant and meaningful Jewish life they can?

As I speak to Jewish leaders all over the country about the subject of next generation Judaism, I note that we are all asking the same questions and that we all have the same fears about the Jewish future. Believe it or not, this fear actually gives me hope. Because the concern is so great, many passionate, thoughtful, and visionary people find themselves working side-by-side to find answers. This book represents one particular vision for a new kind of Jewish organization that can run two different operating systems simultaneously. While the models that work on a college campus may not translate seamlessly to the adult Jewish community, the purpose of the book is to provoke a conversation about the future that is important and in many ways urgent. When I have shared these ideas either in a presentation or through a consulting project, I have been overwhelmed by how the energy in the room transforms. What starts as conversation about how to fix what's wrong grows into a positive, enthusiastic, and visionary conversation about how to reimagine what our work and our community can look like. This book is not a survey of current research or an objective study by an empirical sociologist. It represents the work of the Hillel movement with a deep focus on one Hillel in particular in order to serve as a conversation starter. In this way, this is not a book to read alone but rather with a larger group of leaders who have the power to make a difference in your communities.

Will the Next Generation Become Post-Institutional?

The question of whether American Jews are really becoming post-institutional is certainly not an easy one to answer. While there is a great deal of evidence that suggests that a large segment of American Jews are becoming post-institutional, the discussion about whether it's true may be irrelevant. Perhaps the power of post-institutional Judaism isn't in naming a trend, but in using the idea as a way of pushing us to think in new ways. What would it look like if we, as organizational leaders, started to act in post-institutional ways? What if we all paused from the busyness of our lives and leadership and asked ourselves a different set of questions? Imagine for a moment if ...

- you didn't have to worry about sustaining and filling a building?
- you didn't have to worry about membership, attendance, or annual donations?
- you could just start a new Jewish organization from scratch and be free from the daily institutional responsibilities that slow your organization down?
- you started your first day at this new organization without "regulars" and you had to go out and build a constituency from the ground up?

How would your work be different than it is today?

The answers to these questions are the starting points for imagining and building a different Jewish future. My guess is that for many of us, the answers to these questions would lead to building and designing jobs and organizations that are structured in a new way and focused on a different set of issues and experiences. And that's part of the problem. So many of us feel stuck. We have so much work to do just to sustain the status quo, but we know deep in our hearts that maintaining the status quo isn't enough to turn things around and inspire a different Jewish future.

While it may be a fantasy for established Jewish organizations to simply stop doing what we're doing and reinvent ourselves in totality, it is *not* a fantasy to figure out ways to make meaningful changes. We can start small, simply by making a few crucial decisions that would free up some time and resources to begin to experiment with new and innovative models for Jewish life.

How to Move Forward

So how do we do this? How do we stop the constant cycle of doing what we *need* to do so that we can focus on what we *ought* to do?

Step #1: Do Some Consciousness Raising

Before we can even begin to change, we need to come to terms with what's working and what's not working. It is nearly impossible to adapt without really understanding how dramatically the world is evolving around us—we need to acquire a deep and intuitive sense of how Judaism and community are changing in our world.

Step #2: See Jews for Who They Really Are

The idea that we are all one Jewish community is no longer helpful. By accepting how different we all are and by understanding how each of us has a different configuration of Jewish intelligences, we free ourselves from the Club Model. Rather than focusing on a one-size-fits-all approach or how to recruit more Jews on the periphery to meet us where we are, we can go out and empower different communities of Jews to be creators of Jewish life for themselves. The more people who own their Judaism both inside and outside of Jewish institutions, the more diverse, vibrant, and accessible Jewish life becomes.

Step #3: Invert the Values Pyramid

We need to find ways to spend at least as much time worrying about how to make a positive difference in people's lives as we do worrying about budgets, membership, and attendance.

Step #4: Get Out of the Building

In addition to focusing on improving the experience of people who show up to events, a key strategy for building Jewish life for the next generation is to go out and bring Jewish life to wherever people live, work, and play. This means more than taking a Torah study class out to a local bar; it means taking the Torah study class out to a new group of people who have yet to be engaged. Before we can plan the Torah study class, we have to do the hard work of building relationship with new people who are part of the vast majority of American Jews we call Engagement Jews, so that they can become co-creators in this new learning community.

Step #5: Create a Model of Disruptive Innovation

Set aside some time, staff, and money to incubate real change. As we learned from the JRP model at Penn Hillel and from the story of Target and Dayton Hudson, it is very hard for establishment organizations to really innovate. The only way to make it happen is for established Jewish organizations to create their own Jewish start-ups and give them room to grow and disrupt without forcing them back into the institutional structure.

Step #6: Stop Focusing on What's Wrong

One of the simplest tools we have to free ourselves from current structures in Jewish organizations is simply to choose a new starting point for our strategic thinking. Rather than starting with what's wrong and what needs to be fixed, we can use the power of asset-based community development theory to focus on what's right. By starting with assets, we can build organizations that are smarter and faster and that actually help create empowered communities rather than individual passive clients.

Step #7: Embrace the Power of Tracking and Data

Once we start focusing on what really matters, the best way to ensure we actually follow through on our goals is to track the right things. The next generation of Jewish organizations will be able to use data to enhance their ability to reach large numbers of people in deep and highly impactful ways. Without real data, we run the risk of a kind of mission creep that leads us to focus on what's urgent rather than what's important.

Step #8: Apply Peer-to-Peer Engagement Methodology

Professionals and people with formal leadership titles cannot do it all. The only way for organizations with limited resources to reach the widest variety of people in the deepest way possible is to unlock the power of social networks and enlist an army of community members who will engage their peers and become creators of Jewish life for their networks.

A Nod to the Future

Whenever I am feeling pessimistic about the future of American Judaism, I just go and spend some time with college students. They are so smart, entrepreneurial, and passionate. Those of us who live in the "real world" are lucky to have such a powerful cohort of leaders in the pipeline. We have a great future ahead of us, if only we can allow ourselves to think beyond survival and to see new and different possibilities for what the matrix of Jewish communities could look like in the next few decades. While it will certainly be different, it may be even better than we can imagine.

Acknowledgments

There are so many people to thank who helped make this book a reality. First and foremost, I want to thank my wife, Leora Eisenstadt, for her incredible intellect and sound judgment, which helped shape and focus the entire project from start to finish. On top of that, she was endlessly patient as I spent too many nights and weekends working on the book rather than being at home and fully engaged in our robust family life. I want to thank my children, Avital, Benny, and Coby, who were also endlessly patient and enthusiastic about this project. I am also deeply appreciative of the support and love of my larger family, including Judy Uram, Earl Cohen, Katie and Zol Eisenstadt, David and Rachel Uram, and Daniel Eisenstadt and Sharon Musher. In particular, I want to thank my mom and Sharon for their comments and editing on the manuscript.

I have been blessed throughout my career with a number of mentors who were as generous as they were gifted in their professional lives. First and foremost among them is Jeremy Brochin, the longtime Hillel director at the University of Pennsylvania. Jeremy played a transformative role in helping me transition from rabbinical school to working on a college campus. Jeremy has always been a thought leader in Hillel's engagement endeavor (reaching out to students who aren't already connected to Hillel), and our conversations in my early years of working at Penn Hillel helped shape and concretize my views about what the next generation of Jewish organizations should look like. In fact, Jeremy helped me craft the very first presentation that became the foundation of this book. Jeremy not only taught me an incredible amount but also, through his listening, support, and positive encouragement, helped me find my own voice. Quite literally, I would not be where I am today without Jeremy as my mentor. I also want to mention my hometown rabbi, Rabbi Daniel

Roberts, who was an important role model for me and endlessly encouraged me to become a rabbi.

There are other mentors and colleagues in the Hillel system who also should be mentioned. Rob Goldberg, who was the Hillel director at Washington University when I was a student, would take me for coffee at a diner near campus, where we would discuss and debate how to "fix the Jewish world" and how to create organizations that could reach every Jew regardless of their background. Rabbi Michael Balinsky was a huge role model for me and was my first supervisor at the Hillel at Northwestern University during my formative year as a Steinhardt Jewish Campus Service Corps Fellow. In addition, there was Scott Brown, Rabbi Jim Diamond z"l, Debbie Yunker Kail, Marla Meyers, Rhoda Weisman, and so many others. In particular, I would like to mention my old roommate at Hillel conferences, Adam Simon. We would stay up late at night thinking deeply about how to change the Jewish future.

I also want to acknowledge specifically my mentor Rabbi Larry Sebert; the origin of this book goes back to when he invited me to present to his rabbinical student seminar at the Jewish Theological Seminary a decade ago.

I want to thank a number of people at Penn Hillel as well. My biggest inspiration and greatest teachers have always been the students on campus. They are smart, visionary, creative, entrepreneurial, and fun. It is a great pleasure and distinct honor to be part of their experience at the University of Pennsylvania.

The vast majority of this book was written during a sabbatical from my Hillel duties. For that time away, I owe a huge debt of gratitude to Rachel Hollander, Rabbi Josh Bolton, and Gina Ceisler Shapiro, who each went above and beyond their daily work schedules to make sure that Penn Hillel was strong while I was away. In addition to the staff, I also want to thank all of the lay leaders who are involved with Penn Hillel, both on the Board of Overseers and on the National Board of Governors.

In particular, I want to thank Ron Perilstein, Jackie Einstein Astrof, Marty Lautman, Julie Platt, and Susanna Lachs Adler. As current and past chairs for both of our boards, these leaders not only helped make the sabbatical possible but have served as wonderful cheerleaders and thought partners throughout the years. Finally, I want to thank Joan Bobroff and Jamie Cohen, who keep me and Penn Hillel running smoothly.

There is also a long list of people who have been great coaches and thought partners, helping make this book possible. They include Fern Chertok, Steven Cohen, Eric Fingerhut, Beth Glick, Rabbi Larry Hoffman, Rabbi Jill Jacobs, Rabbi Elie Kaunfer, Rae Ringel, Rabbi Danya Ruttenberg, Len Saxe, and Rabbi Jessica Zimmerman Graf. I want to make special mention of Rabbi Marc Wolf at the Shalom Hartman Institute of North America for helping me find additional Jewish sources to place throughout the book.

Michael Steinhardt has also played an influential role in the development of this book, not just because of his encouragement for the project, but also because his philanthropy has shaped my whole professional experience, starting with the Steinhardt JCSC Fellowship, through the Steinhardt Scholars program, until today when I spend most of my days working in Steinhardt Hall, the home of Penn Hillel.

I want to thank a number of people who served as readers for the project along the way, including Chancellor Arnie Eisen, Adam Simon, David Trietsch, Judy Uram, Ron Wolfson, and Jen Zwilling. I want to thank Warren Hoffman for his loving but tough criticism. He was right, and he offered this criticism at a pivotal time in the writing process.

I want to thank Alys Yablon Wylen for her fantastic editing and Dina Blechman for her work as a research assistant and early editor. I want to thank Stuart M. Matlins, Emily Wichland, and Rachel Shields at Jewish Lights for supporting this book and for generously helping me to become an author.

There is a group of friends and colleagues who were part of the "Partnership Gatherings" instigated by Hillel International and the Jim Joseph Foundation. The group began meeting just before I took over as the director of Penn Hillel, and it was at these discussions that I found my voice for the next chapter of my career in Hillel. I owe a debt to this group for some of the ideas contained in this book, both because they were my teachers and my sounding board. The group was a brilliant and creative bunch of Hillel directors, including David Rittberg, Rabbi Ari Israel, Rabbi Jeffrey Summit, Rabbi David Komerofsky, Joseph Kohane,

Jay Lewis, Hal Ossman, Rabbi Chaim Seidler-Feller, Rabbi Will Berkowitz, and Dan Liebenson. Graham Hoffman and Beth Cousens from Hillel International were essential parts of the group as well. I want to offer a special thanks to Jen Zwilling, whose profound leadership and facilitation created the space for these transformative conversations.

Finally, I want to thank the colleagues who were willing to contribute essays to the book: Rabbi Sharon Brous, Rabbi Noah Farkas, Rabbi Josh Heller, Yehudah Kurtzer, Rabbi Joel Nickerson, Rabbi Alan Silverstein, and Rabbi Dan Smokler.

Notes

Foreword

1. Pew Research Center's Religion & Public Life Project, *A Portrait of Jewish Americans: Findings from a Pew Research Center Survey of U.S. Jews* (Washington, DC: Pew Research Center, 2013).

Introduction

1. I am grateful to Rabbi Irwin Kula, who shared this idea with me during one of our early conversations.

2. Alicia Cohen, "Lessons from the JCSC Fellowship: Professional Development for New Professionals," *Journal of Jewish Communal Service* 84, no. 3/4 (Summer/Fall 2009): 353–360.

3. Roger Bennett, Erin Potts, Rachel Levin, and Stacy Abramson, "*Grande Soy Vanilla Latte with Cinnamon, No Foam ...*": Jewish Identity and Community in a Time of Unlimited Choices (Reboot, April 1, 2006), 21, www.bjpa.org /Publications/details.cfm?PublicationID=329.

4. While many of these features still exist in Orthodox communities, they are starting to change among millennials who are Modern Orthodox.

5. Steven M. Cohen and Arnold M. Eisen, *The Jew Within: Self, Family, and Community in America* (Bloomington: Indiana University Press, 2000), 183.

6. While it is impossible to know exactly what percentage of North American Jews are Empowerment Jews versus Engagement Jews, I want to share just a few statistics that might shape our understanding of how many people fit in each category. We often think that having a bar or bat mitzvah ceremony is a ubiquitous Jewish experience, yet only 51 percent of Jews in the United States chose to participate in this life-cycle event. As I describe the difference between Engagement and Empowerment Jews here and later in chapter 2, think about the different *b'nei mitzvah* ceremonies you've been to, and consider who you would put in each category. A few other statistics that might be helpful include the fact that only 31 percent of American Jews belong to synagogues and only 18 percent belong to some other type of Jewish organization (and we can safely assume that there is a lot of overlap among these populations). Again, while it may be impossible to arrive at some definitive statistic,

it is safe to assume that the majority of Jews in American are not as engaged and active in Jewish life as they could be.

7. While there are many traditions about the origins of this quote, it seems that it was coined by Henry Ford and popularized by Tony Robbins (and Rae Ringel).

Chapter 1: Meet the Millennials

1. This is true for the liberal movements (including Reform, Conservative, and Reconstructionist Judaism). The dynamic for Orthodox synagogues is different. In many places, Orthodoxy is growing and bucking this trend.

2. Pew Research Center's Religion & Public Life Project, *A Portrait of Jewish Americans: Findings from a Pew Research Center Survey of U.S. Jews* (Washington, DC: Pew Research Center, 2013), 12, www.pewforum.org/2013/10/01/jewish-american-beliefs-attitudes-culture-survey/.

3. Pew Research Center's Religion & Public Life Project, *"Nones" on the Rise* (Washington, DC: Pew Research Center, 2012), 9, www.pewforum.org/2012/10/09/nones-on-the-rise/.

4. This is based on anecdotal evidence gathered through nearly one thousand Birthright interviews conducted by Penn Hillel between 2005 and 2016.

5. Pew Research Center's Religion & Public Life Project, *"Nones" on the Rise*, 9–10.

6. Ibid., 22–23; Pew Research Center's Religion & Public Life Project, *A Portrait of Jewish Americans*, 13.

7. The phrase comes from the penultimate verse of Gordon's poem "Hakitzah ami" (Awake My People!); *YIVO Encyclopedia of Jews in Eastern Europe*, s.v. "Gordon, Yehudah Leib," www.yivoencyclopedia.org/article.aspx/Gordon_Yehudah_Leib.

8. It is important to underscore here that of course anti-Semitism still exists in potent ways in America. That said, it functions differently than it did for past generations. Today's young Jews are not being barred from certain professions, social clubs, and universities like they might have been in the middle part of the twentieth century.

9. Pew Research Center's Religion & Public Life Project, *A Portrait of Jewish Americans*, 45.

10. Tzvi Blanchard, "How to Think About Being Jewish in the Twenty-First Century: A New Model of Jewish Identity Construction," *Journal of Jewish Communal Service* 70, no. 1 (Fall 2002): 38.

11. Isa Aron and Lawrence A. Hoffman, *Becoming a Congregation of Learners: Learning as a Key to Revitalizing Congregational Life* (Woodstock, VT: Jewish Lights, 2000), 14.

12. Ibid., 16.

13. Robert D. Putnam, *Bowling Alone: The Collapse and Revival of American Community* (New York: Simon & Schuster, 2001), 42.

14. Pew Research Center's Religion & Public Life Project, *"Nones" on the Rise*, 7.

15. Clay Shirky, *Here Comes Everybody: The Power of Organizing Without Organizations*, reprint ed. (New York: Penguin Books, 2009), 55–61.

16. Pew Research Center's Religion & Public Life Project, *A Portrait of Jewish Americans*, 15.

17. "Millennials vs. Earlier Generations: A Scorecard," *Atlantic Video*, April 25, 2013, www.theatlantic.com/video/index/275049/millennials-vs-earlier-generations-a-scorecard/.

18. Claire Raines and Arleen Arnsparger, "Millennials at Work," *Generations at Work*, March 20, 2010, www.generationsatwork.com/millennials-at-work/.

19. Kim Severson, "Cereal, a Taste of Nostalgia, Looks for Its Next Chapter," *New York Times*, February 22, 2016, www.nytimes.com/2016/02/24/dining/breakfast-cereal.html.

20. T. Scott Gross, "Portrait of a Millennial," *Forbes*, June 27, 2012, www.forbes.com/sites/prospernow/2012/06/27/portrait-of-a-millennial-2/#139c734cacf9.

21. Ibid.

22. Raines and Arnsparger, "Millennials at Work."

23. Pew Research Center's Social & Demographic Trends Project, *Millennials in Adulthood* (Washington, DC: Pew Research Center, 2014), 7.

24. Hartman Group, "Five Things You Need to Know About Millennials," *Heartbeat Newsletter*, February 26, 2013, www.hartman-group.com/hartbeat/463/five-things-you-need-to-know-about-millennials.

25. Ibid.

26. Fern Chertok, Theodore Sasson, and Leonard Saxe, *Tourists, Travelers, and Citizens: Jewish Engagement of Young Adults in Four Centers of North American Jewish Life* (Waltham, MA: Maurice and Marilyn Cohen Center for Modern Jewish Studies, Brandeis University, March 2009), 6, www.brandeis.edu/cmjs/noteworthy/tourists.html.

27. Ibid., 27–28.

28. Cohen and Eisen, *The Jew Within*, 184–85.

29. Chertok, Sasson, and Saxe, *Tourists, Travelers, and Citizens*, 2.

30. Mark Penn and E. Kinney Zalesne, *Microtrends: The Small Forces Behind Tomorrow's Big Changes*, reprint ed. (New York: Twelve, 2009), xviii.

31. Chertok, Sasson, and Saxe, *Tourists, Travelers, and Citizens*, 29.

32. Sherry Turkle, "Cyberspace and Identity," *Contemporary Sociology* 28, no. 6 (November 1999): 643.

33. Theodore Sasson, Leonard Saxe, Fern Chertok, Michelle Shain, Shahar Hecht, and Graham Wright, *Millennial Children of Intermarriage: Touchpoints and*

Trajectories of Jewish Engagement (Waltham, MA: Maurice and Marilyn Cohen Center for Modern Jewish Studies, Brandeis University, October 2015), 5.

34. *The National Jewish Population Survey Results 2000–01: Strength, Challenge and Diversity in the American Jewish Population* (New York: United Jewish Communities, 2003, updated 2004), www.jewishdatabank.org/studies /downloadFile.cfm?FileID=1490.

35. Theodore Sasson, "New Analysis of Pew Data: Children of Intermarriage Increasingly Identify as Jews," *Tablet*, November 11, 2013, www.tabletmag.com /jewishnews-and-politics/151506/young-jews-opt-in.

36. Eleanor Barkhorn, "Getting Married Later Is Great for College-Educated Women," *Atlantic*, March 25, 2015, www.theatlantic.com/sexes /archive/2013/03/getting-married-later-is-great-for-college-educated-women /274040/.

37. Leonard Saxe, Michelle Shain, Graham Wright, Shahar Hecht, Shira Fishman, and Theodore Sasson, *Jewish Futures Project* (Waltham, MA: Maurice and Marilyn Cohen Center for Modern Jewish Studies at Brandeis University, October 2012), www.brandeis.edu/cmjs/researchprojects/jewishfutures /index.html. In addition to this study, Professor Leonard Saxe shared with me a yet unpublished report based on the same data that suggests that only 50 percent of American Jews are married by age thirty-one.

38. Jeffrey Arnett, "Emerging Adulthood: A Theory of Development from the Late Teens through the Twenties," *American Psychologist* 55, no. 5 (May 2000): 469.

39. David Brooks, "The Odyssey Years," *New York Times*, October 9, 2007. www.nytimes.com/2007/10/09/opinion/09brooks.html.

40. There are of course some organizations doing good work to engage Jews in this age group. Moishe House is just one example of an organization standing in this gap.

Chapter 2: We Are More Than One Jewish People

1. Theodore Sasson, Leonard Saxe, Fern Chertok, Michelle Shain, Shahar Hecht, and Graham Wright, *Millennial Children of Intermarriage: Touchpoints and Trajectories of Jewish Engagement* (Waltham, MA: Maurice and Marilyn Cohen Center for Modern Jewish Studies, Brandeis University, October 2015), 5.

2. Ron Wolfson, *Relational Judaism: Using the Power of Relationships to Transform the Jewish Community* (Woodstock, VT: Jewish Lights, 2013), 53.

3. Steven M. Cohen and Arnold M. Eisen, *The Jew Within: Self, Family, and Community in America* (Bloomington: Indiana University Press, 2000), 185.

4. Ibid., 182.

5. Lawrence A. Hoffman, *Rethinking Synagogues: A New Vocabulary for Congregational Life* (Woodstock, VT: Jewish Lights, 2006), 21.

6. Isa Aron, Steven M. Cohen, Lawrence A. Hoffman, and Ari Y. Kelman, *Sacred Strategies: Transforming Synagogues from Functional to Visionary* (Herndon, VA: Rowman & Littlefield, 2010), 3; Cohen and Eisen, *The Jew Within*, 16.

7. At first glance it might seem that by measuring higher and lower levels of Jewish association, I am breaking my own rule and ranking Jews on some kind of hierarchical and judgmental spectrum. The difference here is that I am not making a judgment about whether higher or lower levels of Jewish association are better or worse. When I use the term "lower level of Jewish association," the goal is not to identify which population needs to be fixed, but only to better understand how to engage them regardless of whether that results in a different level of Jewish association.

8. The theory of multiple intelligences was developed in 1983 by Dr. Howard Gardner, professor of education at Harvard University. It suggests that the traditional notion of intelligence, based on IQ testing, is far too limited. Other forms of intelligence like musical, visual, verbal, logical, kinesthetic, and emotional all need to be taken into account as well.

9. While our initial motivation was the idea of multiple Jewish intelligences, this model also borrows from the Myers-Briggs personality inventory, which measures personality types based on four dichotomies.

Chapter 3: Seeding Change from Within

1. I want to express a special thank you to a good friend and thought partner, Dan Libenson, founder and president of the Institute for the Next Jewish Future and director of jU Chicago, who first introduced me to these ideas.

2. Avi Dan, "The Death of Scale: Is Kodak's Failure an Omen of Things to Come for Corporate America?," *Forbes*, August 20, 2013, www.forbes.com/sites/avidan/2013/08/20/the-death-of-scale-is-kodaks-failure-an-omen-of-things-to-come-for-corporate-america/#3447b6602549.

3. Clayton M. Christensen, *The Innovator's Dilemma: The Revolutionary Book That Will Change the Way You Do Business*, reprint ed. (New York: Harper Business, 2011), 112.

4. "Disruptive Technology/Innovation," *Economist*, May 11, 2009, www.economist.com/node/13636558.

5. Clayton M. Christensen, Michael E. Raynor, and Rory McDonald, "What Is Disruptive Innovation?," *Harvard Business Review*, December 2015, https://hbr.org/2015/12/what-is-disruptive-innovation.

6. Stephen Witt, "The Man Who Broke the Music Business," *New Yorker*, April 27, 2015, www.newyorker.com/magazine/2015/04/27/the-man-who-broke-the-music-business.

7. Christensen, *The Innovator's Dilemma*, 117.

8. Ibid., 113.

9. Ibid.

10. Steven M. Cohen and Arnold M. Eisen, *The Jew Within: Self, Family, and Community in America* (Bloomington: Indiana University Press, 2000), 13.

11. Christensen, *The Innovator's Dilemma*, xxiv.

12. Oded Shenkar, *Copycats: How Smart Companies Use Imitation to Gain a Strategic Edge* (Boston: Harvard Business Review Press, 2010), 93.

13. Christensen, *The Innovator's Dilemma*, 131.

14. Ibid.

15. "Target Annual Report: 2014," 2015, http://corporate.target.com/annual-reports /2014/download.

Chapter 4: Disruptive Innovation at Penn Hillel

1. Beth Kanter, Allison Fine, and Randi Zuckerberg, *The Networked Nonprofit: Connecting with Social Media to Drive Change* (San Francisco: Jossey-Bass, 2010), 66.

2. Joel Nickerson called this shedding their pediatric understanding of Judaism. This is not just for college students; many adults are also limited in their ability to appreciate and experience Jewish life because they are still challenged by a pediatric understanding of Judaism.

3. Isa Aron, Steven M. Cohen, Lawrence A. Hoffman, and Ari Y. Kelman, *Sacred Strategies: Transforming Synagogues from Functional to Visionary* (Herndon, VA: Rowman & Littlefield, 2010), 8.

4. Malcolm Gladwell, *The Tipping Point: How Little Things Can Make a Big Difference* (Boston: Back Bay Books, 2002), 15–29.

5. Ibid., 3-4.

6. In the first iterations of JRP, the job descriptions of staff were more focused on inspiring students to plan programs for their friends. Graham Hoffman (associate vice president for Strategy, 2003–2014), Jen Zwilling (vice president for Strategy and Measurement, 2004–), and others at Hillel International helped develop this idea further in a way that placed the central focus of engagement professionals on building relationships with 180 students.

7. Steven M. Cohen, Ezra Kopelowitz, Jack Ukeles, and Minna Wolf, *"Assessing the Impact of Senior Jewish Educators and Campus Entrepreneurs Initiative Interns on the Jewish Engagement of College Students—Two Year Summary: 2008–2010* (Hillel International and the Jim Joseph Foundation, November 2, 2010), 18.

8. We chose these Jewish expressions to create a simple baseline for students who have little to no institutional experience.

9. Gladwell, *The Tipping Point*, 30–88.

10. This is also a common practice in the Orthodox Jewish outreach world. Many of the outreach rabbis working on campus today didn't grow up "religious" but became *baal teshuvah* (newly religious) later in life.

Chapter 5: Moving from Clubs to Networks

1. The basis of images used here were developed by Simon Amiel (director of the Steinhardt JCSC Fellowship, 2004–2007) and Graham Hoffman (associate vice president for Strategy, 2003–2014) with help from Claire Goldwater (director of the Meyerhoff Center for Jewish Experience, 2004–2009).

2. Steven M. Cohen and Ari Y. Kelman, *Cultural Events and Jewish Identities: Young Adult Jews in New York* (New York: UJA-Federation of New York, February 2005), www.bjpa.org/Publications/details.cfm?PublicationID=2911, 5.

3. Ruth Balinsky Friedman, "When You're Facing Infertility, a Synagogue Can Be the Most Painful Place to Go. Let's Change That," *Washington Post*, March 30, 2016, www.washingtonpost.com/news/acts-of-faith/wp/2016/03/30/when-youre-facing-infertility-a-synagogue-can-be-the-most-painful-place-to-go-lets-change-that/.

4. I borrow the term Jewish "segmentation" here from a talk that I heard Leonard Fein give years ago. While the terminology stuck, the exact source didn't.

5. Steven M. Cohen and Arnold M. Eisen, *The Jew Within: Self, Family, and Community in America* (Bloomington: Indiana University Press, 2000), 184.

6. Ron Wolfson, *Relational Judaism: Using the Power of Relationships to Transform the Jewish Community* (Woodstock, VT: Jewish Lights, 2013), 41.

7. John P. Kretzmann and John L. McKnight, *Building Communities from the Inside Out: A Path Toward Finding and Mobilizing a Community's Assets* (Evanston, IL: ACTA Publications, 1993), 5.

8. Isa Aron, Steven M. Cohen, Lawrence A. Hoffman, and Ari Y. Kelman, *Sacred Strategies: Transforming Synagogues from Functional to Visionary* (Herndon, VA: Rowman & Littlefield, 2010), 19.

9. Graham Hoffman, "Networks and Community," convening of the Jim Joseph Major grantees, July 21, 2009.

10. Clay Shirky, *Here Comes Everybody: The Power of Organizing Without Organizations*, reprint ed. (New York: Penguin Books, 2009), 214ff.

11. Ibid., 216, 220.

12. Ibid., 221.

13. Malcolm Gladwell, "The Cellular Church: How Rick Warren's Congregation Grew," *New Yorker*, September 12, 2005, www.newyorker.com/magazine/2005/09/12/the-cellular-church.

14. Shirky, *Here Comes Everybody*, 222.

15. Ibid.

Chapter 6: Building an Impact Organization

1. Isa Aron, Steven M. Cohen, Lawrence A. Hoffman, and Ari Y. Kelman, *Sacred Strategies: Transforming Synagogues from Functional to Visionary* (Herndon, VA: Rowman & Littlefield, 2010), 21.

2. Leslie R. Crutchfield, Heather McLeod Grant, and J. Gregory Dees, *Forces for Good* (San Francisco: Jossey-Bass, 2008), 18.

3. Aron et al., *Sacred Strategies*, 19.

4. Ron Wolfson, *Relational Judaism: Using the Power of Relationships to Transform the Jewish Community* (Woodstock, VT: Jewish Lights, 2013), 22.

5. Beth Kanter, Allison Fine, and Randi Zuckerberg, *The Networked Nonprofit: Connecting with Social Media to Drive Change* (San Francisco: Jossey-Bass, 2010), 93.

6. Aron et al., *Sacred Strategies*, 143.

7. Lawrence A. Hoffman, *Rethinking Synagogues: A New Vocabulary for Congregational Life* (Woodstock, VT: Jewish Lights, 2006), 35.

8. These mechanisms can be simple. Rather than hosting a speaker as a "one-off" event, it can be constructed as a speaker series with incentives for people to attend the whole series and with small-group table discussions groups after to build more community. Ideally, there is also a plan for how to follow up with each of the new people so that they can be connected to the next set of relationships and Jewish experiences.

9. Jacobellis v. Ohio, 378 U.S. 184 (1964) at 197 (Stewart, J., concurring).

10. These problems are often compounded by the fact that even when small organizations collect good data, they do not have the infrastructure and expertise necessary to analyze that data in a way that generates useful information.

11. Hoffman, *Rethinking Synagogues*, 19.

12. Beth Cousens, "REACH Jewish Growth Outcomes," internal report for Hillel International, June 2, 2010. The origin of the four bubbles comes from Graham Hoffman (associate vice president for strategy, 2003–2014) with help from Claire Goldwater (director of the Meyerhoff Center for Jewish Experience, 2004–2009).

13. Steven M. Cohen and Arnold M. Eisen, *The Jew Within: Self, Family, and Community in America* (Bloomington: Indiana University Press, 2000), 13.

14. Ibid., 41.

15. CEI is the Hillel International adaptation of a initiative that had existed at Penn Hillel since the late 1990s. Hillel International developed it in important ways. Through the generous support of the Jim Joseph Foundation and other Hillel International grant money, a form of peer-to-peer engagement now exists on dozens of campus around the country.

Chapter 7: An Educational Philosophy for Impact Organizations

1. Isa Aron, Steven M. Cohen, Lawrence A. Hoffman, and Ari Y. Kelman, *Sacred Strategies: Transforming Synagogues from Functional to Visionary* (Herndon, VA: Rowman & Littlefield, 2010), 17. This is one of several places in this books that argues that Jewish organizations need to move away from what Larry Hoffman calls "limited liability communities," which specialize in providing

well-refined services or programs without a serious focus on trying to make a deep and transformative impact on the lives of the people they serve.

2. While we had read other works by Parker Palmer, Rabbi Dan Smokler first introduced Penn Hillel to *A Hidden Wholeness*. It was also Rabbi Smokler who first sparked our thinking about how to apply it to the Hillel context.

3. Parker J. Palmer, *A Hidden Wholeness: The Journey Toward an Undivided Life* (San Francisco: Jossey-Bass, 2009), 92.

4. Ibid., 92–93.

5. This is an idea and methodology that my mother-in-law, Dr. Katie Eisenstadt, has perfected in her work as a therapist and parenting expert.

6. Palmer, *A Hidden Wholeness*, 92–93.

7. Franz Rosenzweig, *On Jewish Learning*, ed. N. N. Glatzer (New York: Schocken Books, 1955), 98.

8. A key catalyst for the development of these ideas was the conversations taking place among a handful of visionary Hillel directors and Hillel International thought leaders, made possible through the funding of the Jim Joseph Foundation.

9. Parker J. Palmer, *The Courage to Teach: Exploring the Inner Landscape of a Teacher's Life*, 10th anniversary ed. (San Francisco: Jossey-Bass, 2007), 2–3.

10. Aron et al., *Sacred Strategies*, 101. Here I am referring to the overemphasis on John Dewey's dictum that experience is the basis of all education.

11. Laurence R. Iannaccone, "Why Strict Churches Are Strong," *American Journal of Sociology* 99, no. 5 (March 1994): 1180–1211.

Chapter 8: Asset-Based Community Development Theory

1. Isa Aron, Steven M. Cohen, Lawrence A. Hoffman, and Ari Y. Kelman, *Sacred Strategies: Transforming Synagogues from Functional to Visionary* (Herndon, VA: Rowman & Littlefield, 2010), 25.

2. John P. Kretzmann and John L. McKnight, *Building Communities from the Inside Out: A Path Toward Finding and Mobilizing a Community's Assets* (Evanston, IL: ACTA Publications, 1993), 2–3.

3. Ibid., 4–5.

4. Beth Kanter, Allison Fine, and Randi Zuckerberg, *The Networked Nonprofit: Connecting with Social Media to Drive Change* (San Francisco: Jossey-Bass, 2010), 25.

5. Ibid., 12.

6. Aron et al., *Sacred Strategies*, 20.

7. Tzvi Blanchard, "How to Think About Being Jewish in the Twenty-First Century: A New Model of Jewish Identity Construction," *Journal of Jewish Communal Service* 70, no. 1 (Fall 2002): 39.

8. Kretzmann and McKnight, *Building Communities from the Inside Out*, 6–10.

9. Valdis Krebs and June Holley, *Building Smart Communities through Network Weaving*, 2006, www.orgnet.com/BuildingNetworks.pdf. See this article for a more thorough discussion of network weaving.

10. Malcolm Gladwell, *The Tipping Point: How Little Things Can Make a Big Difference* (Boston: Back Bay Books, 2002), 61–62 for mavens, 68–69 for connectors, and 78–80 for salesmen.

11. Kretzmann and McKnight, *Building Communities from the Inside Out*, 5.

12. Keith Hampton, Lauren Sessions Goulet, Eun Ja Her, and Lee Rainie, *Social Isolation and New Technology* (Washington, DC: Pew Research Center, 2009), www.pewinternet.org/2009/11/04/social-isolation-and-new-technology/.

13. Google My Maps, https://www.google.com/maps/d/.

14. Kanter, Fine, and Zuckerberg, *The Networked Nonprofit*, 3–4.

15. I learned about this kind of resource sharing from a brilliant and creative lay leader in northern New Jersey named Julie Eisen. See the following website for information about the details of this highly successful program: www.jfnnj.org/kehillahcooperative.

16. Just a simple search on Google or crowdsourcing the question to Facebook reveals that this is happening in large and small ways in many regions of the country. The problem with most of the examples that I have found is that organizations are starting to partner and merge not as a proactive strategy to find better ways of making a positive impact in the communities they work with, but rather as a last ditch effort to solve deep and complicated problems related to shrinking communities and an overabundance of infrastructure.

17. Aron et al., *Sacred Strategies*, 39.

18. Kanter, Fine, and Zuckerberg, *The Networked Nonprofit*, 25.

19. Adam Simon has a great model for this idea. He sees this as a three-step process moving from consumers, to supported creators, to self-directed creators.

Chapter 9: Peer-to-Peer Engagement

1. Isa Aron, Steven M. Cohen, Lawrence A. Hoffman, and Ari Y. Kelman, *Sacred Strategies: Transforming Synagogues from Functional to Visionary* (Herndon, VA: Rowman & Littlefield, 2010), 133.

2. Ron Wolfson, *Relational Judaism: Using the Power of Relationships to Transform the Jewish Community* (Woodstock, VT: Jewish Lights, 2013), 22, 89.

3. Marshall Ganz, "What Is Public Narrative?" (Kennedy School, 2007), http://chutzpahportfolio.yolasite.com/resources/WhatIsPublicNarrative08.pdf, 3.

4. Peter M. Senge, "The Leader's New Work: Building Learning Organizations," *Sloan Management Review* 32, no. 1 (Fall 1990). Senge is talking about this concept as it relates to leadership, but it also provides a powerful analogy for the work of a peer engager.

5. Ganz, "What Is Public Narrative?," 3.

6. Ibid., 9–15.

7. Wolfson, *Relational Judaism*, 100.

8. Ibid.

9. Steven M. Cohen, Ezra Kopelowitz, Jack Ukeles, and Minna Wolf, *Assessing the Impact of Senior Jewish Educators and Campus Entrepreneurs Initiative Interns on the Jewish Engagement of College Students—Two-Year Summary: 2008–2010* (Hillel International and the Jim Joseph Foundation, November 2, 2010), 4.

10. Ibid., 18.

11. Ibid., 16.

12. Aron et al., *Sacred Strategies*, 133.

13. Joel Nickerson, "The Art of the (Initial) Jewish Conversation: One Approach to Deep, Meaningful Conversation with Emerging Adults" (Hillel International and Penn Hillel, May 2011).

14. Ibid.

15. Ibid.

16. Steven M. Cohen and Arnold M. Eisen, *The Jew Within: Self, Family, and Community in America* (Bloomington: Indiana University Press, 2000), 15.

17. Hart is now the director of Heart to Heart, http://theheart2heartproject.org/.

18. All too often synagogues think that they have accomplished this because some leader makes an announcement like "We are always looking for new people to lead in our service; please let any of the officers or clergy know if you're interested." It's like the old joke about someone who says to you, "You're welcome for Shabbat at my house any time," because an open invitation is really not an invitation at all. It shifts responsibility from the host to the guest by saying, "You let me know when you want to have Shabbat dinner." The same rule applies when trying to engage a new person. There is a world of difference between saying "Let me know if you're interested" and "Will you read Torah next month, and can we sit down next week to go over it?"

19. Lisa Foster, *Effectiveness of Mentor Programs: Review of the Literature from 1995 to 2000* (Sacramento: California State Library, California Research Bureau 2001), 14.

20. Relational Managing System, http://templerms.com.

21. Hineynu, www.hineynu.com.

22. Roger Bennett, Erin Potts, Rachel Levin, and Stacy Abramson, *"Grande Soy Vanilla Latte with Cinnamon, No Foam ...": Jewish Identity and Community in a Time of Unlimited Choices* (Reboot, April 2006), 23–24.

23. This model was originally developed to describe the art of fund-raising by an exceptional Jewish fund-raising professional named Joy Dawn Prevor, who worked for Hillel International for a time.

24. Wolfson, *Relational Judaism*, 60.

25. Different organizations can define this term for themselves. A simple definition could be to include all people with leadership positions or who participate in your organization's activities once a month or more.

Conclusion

1. If you read the plain text of the Torah, the commandment to build the *Mishkan* comes in Exodus 25:8, well before the sin of the Golden Calf, which takes place in Exodus 32:1. This chronology, however, is inverted by the medieval Jewish commentator Ramban (see his comment on Exodus 25:1), who believes that the commandment to build the *Mishkan* comes after the sin of the Golden Calf. According to Ramban's reading, it is easier to see God's permission to build the *Mishkan* as a kind of accommodation for the Children of Israel, who seem to need material accoutrements to help them feel close to God.

2. Avivah Gottlieb Zornberg, *The Particulars of Rapture: Reflections on Exodus*, reprint ed. (New York: Schocken Books, 2011), 330. Zornberg is quoting *Or HaChaim* 32:11.

3. Yeshayahu Leibowitz, *Judaism, Human Values, and the Jewish State*, ed. Eliezer Goldman, trans. Yoram Navon, Zvi Jacobson, Gershon Levi, and Raphael Levy, rev. ed. (Cambridge, MA: Harvard University Press, 1995), 85–87.

Suggestions for Further Reading

Aron, Isa, Steven M. Cohen, Lawrence A. Hoffman, and Ari Y. Kelman. *Sacred Strategies: Transforming Synagogues from Functional to Visionary.* Herndon, VA: Rowman & Littlefield, 2010.

Aron, Isa, and Lawrence A. Hoffman. *Becoming a Congregation of Learners: Learning as a Key to Revitalizing Congregational Life.* Woodstock, VT: Jewish Lights, 2000.

Bennett, Roger, Erin Potts, Rachel Levin, and Stacy Abramson. *"Grande Soy Vanilla Latte with Cinnamon, No Foam ...": Jewish Identity and Community in a Time of Unlimited Choices.* Reboot, April 1, 2006. www.bjpa.org/Publications /details.cfm?PublicationID=329.

Blanchard, Tzvi. "How to Think about Being Jewish in the Twenty-First Century: A New Model of Jewish Identity Construction." *Journal of Jewish Communal Service* 70, no. 1 (Fall 2002).

Chertok, Fern, Theodore Sasson, and Leonard Saxe. *Tourists, Travelers, and Citizens: Jewish Engagement of Young Adults in Four Centers of North American Jewish Life.* Waltham, MA: Maurice and Marilyn Cohen Center for Modern Jewish Studies, Brandeis University, March 2009. www.brandeis.edu/cmjs /noteworthy/tourists.html.

Christensen, Clayton M. *The Innovator's Dilemma: The Revolutionary Book That Will Change the Way You Do Business.* Reprint ed. New York: Harper Business, 2011.

Cohen, Steven M., and Arnold M. Eisen. *The Jew Within: Self, Family, and Community in America.* Bloomington: Indiana University Press, 2000.

Cohen, Steven M., and Ari Y. Kelman. *Beyond Distancing: Young Adult American Jews and Their Alienation from Israel.* Jewish Identity Project of Reboot, 2007. www.bjpa.org/Publications/details.cfm?PublicationID=326.

Crutchfield, Leslie R., Heather McLeod Grant, and J. Gregory Dees. *Forces for Good: The Six Practices of High-Impact Nonprofits.* 2nd ed. San Francisco: Jossey-Bass, 2012.

Gladwell, Malcolm. *The Tipping Point: How Little Things Can Make a Big Difference*. Boston: Back Bay Books, 2002.

Hoffman, Lawrence A. *Rethinking Synagogues: A New Vocabulary for Congregational Life*. Woodstock, VT: Jewish Lights, 2006.

Kanter, Beth, Allison Fine, and Randi Zuckerberg. *The Networked Nonprofit: Connecting with Social Media to Drive Change*. San Francisco: Jossey-Bass, 2010.

Krebs, Valdis, and June Holley. *Building Smart Communities through Network Weaving*. Appalachian Center for Economic Networks, 2006. www.orgnet.com /BuildingNetworks.pdf.

Kretzmann, John P., and John L. McKnight. *Building Communities from the Inside Out: A Path Toward Finding and Mobilizing a Community's Assets*. Evanston, IL: ACTA Publications, 1993.

Palmer, Parker J. *The Courage to Teach: Exploring the Inner Landscape of a Teacher's Life*. 10th anniversary ed. San Francisco: Jossey-Bass, 2007.

———. *A Hidden Wholeness: The Journey Toward an Undivided Life*. San Francisco: Jossey-Bass, 2009.

Penn, Mark, and E. Kinney Zalesne. *Microtrends: The Small Forces Behind Tomorrow's Big Changes*. Reprint ed. New York: Twelve, 2009.

Pew Research Center's Religion & Public Life Project. *"Nones" on the Rise*. Washington, DC: Pew Research Center, 2012. www.pewforum.org/2012/10/09 /nones-on-the-rise/.

———. *A Portrait of Jewish Americans: Findings from a Pew Research Center Survey of U.S. Jews*. Washington, DC: Pew Research Center, 2013. www.pewforum.org/2013/10/01/jewish-american-beliefs-attitudes-culture-survey/.

Shirky, Clay. *Here Comes Everybody: The Power of Organizing Without Organizations*. Reprint ed. New York: Penguin Books, 2009.

Schwartz, Sidney. *Jewish Megatrends: Charting the Course of the American Jewish Future*. Woodstock, VT: Jewish Lights, 2013.

Wolfson, Ron. *Relational Judaism: Using the Power of Relationships to Transform the Jewish Community*. Woodstock, VT: Jewish Lights, 2013.

CPSIA information can be obtained
at www.ICGtesting.com
Printed in the USA
LVHW11s1442181018
594037LV00002B/356/P